UNDERSTANDING ANXIETY

UNDERSTANDING
Anxiety

Dick Whitehouse
and
Gwyn Devey

Aylesbury, Bucks, HP22 5BL
England

Copyright © Dick Whitehouse & Gwyn Devey 1996
The right of Dick Whitehouse and Gwyn Devey to be identified
as joint authors of this book has been asserted
by them in accordance with the
Copyright, Design and Patents Act 1988.

First published 1996
Alpha, Aylesbury, Bucks HP22 5BL

Book concept, Design and Production
Copyright © Gazelle Books 1996
the publishing imprint of Nuprint Ltd

ISBN 1 898938 26 1

Unless otherwise stated, Scripture quotations
are taken from New International Version (NIV) © 1973, 1978, 1984
by International Bible Society, used by permission of
Zondervan Publishing House and Hodder & Stoughton.

British Library Cataloguing in Publication Data.
A catalogue record for this book is available from
the British Library.

Designed and Produced in England for
ALPHA an imprint of
SP Trust Ltd, Wendover Road, Stoke Mandeville,
Aylesbury, Bucks. HP22 5BL by
Nuprint Ltd, Station Road, Harpenden, Herts AL5 4SE.

Contents

Acknowledgements

We would like to thank our wives, Lorna Devey and Margaret Whitehouse for their patience during the long process of developing this book. In addition to putting up with our absences on long conferences on the material, their shrewd observations and unwillingness to let us get away with half truths, have been a spur to expressing our ideas adequately.

Our thanks also go to the congregations with which we have worked over the years and, in particular to those who have entrusted their counselling confidences to us. The case studies in this book are all based on real events although details have occasionally been changed. Of course, names have been changed in order to protect the innocent and the guilty!

Finally, we wish to thank Ann Ziomek, who typed the first drafts, and the editorial staff at Nuprint who have been a constant encouragement to us in an endeavour which we at times thought would never see the light of day.

Foreword

I first read 'Understanding Anxiety' during a speaking trip I recently made overseas — the reason for this was not because I am an anxious traveller but because the publishers were pressing me for my comments on the book and I was woefully behind schedule.

Before leaving home I had been assured that my travel documents were in order but when I reached my destination it rapidly became clear that they were not. Enduring an extremely inconvenient and humiliating two hour delay in the custody of the immigration officers I was consoled to find this book still with me and reading through, found its message very appropriate! At one stage they were seriously considering sending me home again but each chapter strengthened my determination to die rather than give in to the anxious thoughts and fears this situation was creating. The authorities were rather bewildered to witness my calm exterior and hear my expressions of patience and were further intrigued when I showed them what I was reading. They allowed me through and the experience was proof positive that this book is a realistic help for anyone wishing to find a godly response to the pressures of living in a stress-filled world.

I deeply appreciated the thoroughly professional and soundly biblical approach of 'Understanding Anxiety'. Dick Whitehouse and Gwyn Devey have worked hard to produce a readable, scripturally sound and culturally relevant book.

It is a timely antidote to the worry with which we all struggle; a practical manual on how to live God's way.

For all who wish to overcome the causes and symptoms of anxiety, this is one of the most informative and useful books I have found. It's bound to help — it did me! I warmly commend it to every reader.

Lyndon Bowring
Care

Introduction

One look at the national medical bill for tranquillisers and anti-depressant drugs is enough to show how prevalent the scourge of anxiety in our society is. Add to that the number of people who go for psychiatric or pastoral counselling help and you will begin to realise the extent of the problem. But these manifestations are probably just the tip of a gigantic iceberg; many people who do not actively seek medical, psychiatric or pastoral help nevertheless suffer from the symptoms of an anxiety epidemic.

As we worked over a number of years with Christians who came to us for counselling and as we observed their personal and congregational behaviour, we became convinced that anxiety was a number one cause for many of the events which we saw and for the ways in which people were handling their problems. As we considered the scenario it became obvious to us that this is not a new situation, many of the characters in the Bible exhibited the same symptoms. Even a casual reading of the Psalms demonstrated how the psalmists responded to personal, political and spiritual pressures. Many of their cries to God are born out of anxiety.

It wasn't until much later that we realised that modern psychology agrees with this prognosis. It was the issue of anxiety which led Siegmund Freud to abandon a purely physiological explanation for mental states in favour of a psychological explanation of human behaviour — even if he saw psychological behaviour as being rooted in physical needs. Indeed, so important did Freud consider the issue that he kept putting off a definitive statement of his views on the issue of anxiety until almost the end of his life.

Of course, Freud rejected spiritual explanations of human behaviour but that does not invalidate everything that he said. His analysis needs to be brought to the more searching test of Scripture and a biblical perspective on the nature of man. Freud's insight that anxiety functions as a warning bell to arouse us to deal with danger is particularly instructive. Seward Hiltner compares the signal which anxiety triggers with an alarm clock. When we respond appropriately to the alarm bell, anxiety has done its work and it shuts off until it is needed again. Chronic or damaging anxiety occurs when the alarm refuses to be shut off after the danger has passed.

The same alarm function of anxiety comes into play when we face physical danger and when the danger is not so much physical as a perceived threat to our emotional or spiritual well being. In the case of the physical threat, the body is mobilised by the alarm to take action either by flight, fight or adaptation. This physical preparation for action on the part of our bodies is triggered or accompanied by emotional sensations. The same mechanism is at work when the threat is in the mental, emotional or spiritual spheres, although it works in reverse. We should not therefore, be surprised if the emotional dangers cause physical reactions.

In this book, we attempt to deal with some of the common origins and consequences of misplaced anxiety from a biblical perspective. The Bible is a rich quarry of human experience which exposes the blemished face of humanity.

The interaction of God and the lives of real people provides us with the true understanding of anxiety, and the means of working it out in today's world.

This book is not a manual of clinical psychology, however, it shows the way through the maze towards the clear ground of peace — the mainstay of a mature faith and to Jesus Christ, the ultimate antidote.

We have included a practical section at the back of the book especially for readers who suffer from anxiety or for those who want further guidance. Happy reading.

Dick Whitehouse
Gwynn Devey

PART
1

DESCRIPTION

What Anxiety Is

1

The Corrosive Emotion

Not long ago, a father shot his two attractive young daughters and his wife before turning the gun on himself. A frantic note was found near to the bodies expressing the man's feelings about the declining moral state of the world into which his girls were growing. He also related his fears about a possible nuclear holocaust and what it might do to his family. 'It is better,' he concluded, 'to end it all in this way, at least we will all go together and I will know how they came to their end.' Anxiety had done its deadly work. To the outsider this may have seemed like a sudden untypical act. No doubt the Coroner's verdict read, 'Unlawful killing and suicide committed whilst the balance of the mind was disturbed.' In reality this tragedy was the conclusion of a long period of bottled up, unexpressed anxiety.

This is an extreme case, but anxiety cripples the spiritual, emotional and even physical well-being of countless people in modern society.

A medical handbook defines anxiety in this way:

> Anxiety is a fear reaction which arises from within. No outside stimulus is necessary. The term is used to represent a displeasurable emotional response which is out of proportion to the fear-producing situation.
>
> *Clinical Management of Behavioral Disorders in Children,*
> Dr Henry Bockwin, Philadelphia, 1954, p 343.

This definition will form part of the basis for examining the state of anxiety and the way in which it works. Anxiety is a corroding emotion which can cause all the springs of our personality to seize up. But it can be counteracted. The first rule in any battle ploy is 'know your enemy'. So, by finding out about the nature of anxiety, we can learn to combat its potentially devastating effects.

FEAR WITHOUT CAUSE?

The foolish thing about anxiety is that it often comes out of the blue — 'no outside stimulus is necessary.' The fact that it is defined as a fear reaction gives us the clue. Anxiety is never uncaused. It is an internalized emotion relating to vague, unspecified, and often unspecifiable, fears. The lack of an external stimulus means that there is no *immediate* cause. This does not mean that there is *no* cause at all. Usually we can trace the cause back to something in the sufferer's past.

For instance, Claire was a member of a church from which several members left, apparently suddenly. There was no acrimony or dispute in the church. In fact, each of the people leaving had perfectly good reasons for going elsewhere. Nevertheless, Claire began to feel uneasy and became fearful for her own position. Her anxiety grew but, since she did not try to communicate it, no one was aware of the depth of her feelings. She started to believe that she was unloved by the congregation and suddenly she too left — retired, hurt.

The immediate circumstances are not sufficient to explain Claire's feelings, nor her action. But her experience of life could point to something. She was cut off from her family who no longer wanted anything to do with her. Her mother had walked out of the home when she was young. Her husband left her for another woman after only a few months of marriage. Naturally, she was suffering from a feeling of rejection. When the other members left her church, the rejection bubbled to the surface, causing her to become anxious. Claire's eventual behaviour could have been avoided if she had learned to analyze events more clearly and if her security had been in God.

GUILT AND ANXIETY

The Bible has a great deal to say about anxiety, both in its teaching and its example. In the Sermon on the Mount, Jesus specified a number of everyday concerns which often make people anxious. He went on to say, 'Seek first his Kingdom and his righteousness and all of these things will be yours as well. Therefore do not be anxious about tomorrow, for tomorrow will be anxious for itself. Let the day's own trouble be sufficient for the day' (Matthew 6:33 – 34, RSV).

Earlier, Jesus had taught his disciples how they should pray, in what we now call The Lord's Prayer. He said, 'give us this day our daily bread'. Recent biblical research has shown that the Greek phrase for 'daily bread' is the same phrase used to refer to a soldier's rations. William Barclay, the noted New Testament scholar, comments that a soldier's or labourer's wages were always paid at the end of *each* day. The reason was to avoid undue anxiety, since the day's wages were needed to purchase the next day's bread. Clearly, Jesus does not want us to be overconcerned about the future. Rather he wants us to seek fresh spiritual, physical and emotional supplies each day, knowing that our commander-King has our needs in mind.

The trouble is that *knowing* we are not meant to be anxious often increases our anxiety. We become anxious about being anxious! This can become a vicious cycle in which an initial mild state of anxiety becomes intensified by guilt about being anxious. When Jesus told us to take no anxious thought for tomorrow, he did not intend to send us on a guilt-trip. His desire was not to condemn us, but to liberate us into a carefree atmosphere of acceptance of the Father's love and provision for our needs.

THAT SURLY FELLOW

The Bible is full of examples of anxiety-creating situations. For instance, there is the occasion when King David and his men are on the run from King Saul. David's company are holed up in the wilderness of Paran. From their hide-out they protect many of the local landowners and their men from being attacked by the Philistines. One of the landowners, Nabal, a very rich man, is courteously approached by David to supply his men with some food. Nabal replies to David's servants, 'Who is David? Who is the son of Jesse? There are many servants nowadays who are breaking away from their masters. Shall I take my bread and my water and my meat that I have killed for my shearers and give to men who come from I do not know where?' (1 Samuel 25:10 – 11, RSV).

Clearly, Nabal is anxious for his property. Perhaps he identifies his status with his property. When our status is challenged, anxiety follows. Nabal feared that David would make impossible demands upon him and take all his personal wealth, whereas, in reality, David had protected and saved it. Nabal's anxious attitude stemmed from his own character. He is variously described as surly, churlish, ill-behaved, mean and bad-tempered. The circumstances, in fact, did not warrant his reaction. But his response was dominated by the word 'my'.

Fortunately, Abigail, his wife knew how to respond and her generous gifts averted David's anger. It is significant that Nabal spent the proceeds of his property on himself. When Abigail told her husband what she had done, the night after a drunken feast, Nabal's anxiety took toll. The Bible records, 'in the morning, when the wine had gone out of Nabal, his wife told him these things and his heart died within him.' Nabal died physically ten days later. There is a deep insight here. The anxious person often dies emotionally before he dies physically. Nabal's anxiety response was embedded deeply in his character.

David was also anxious, but he was anxious for his men. However, when he receives Nabal's reply his anxiety explodes into anger — as anxiety often does. He feels like killing Nabal and his men. Abigail not only averts reprisals upon her husband, she also prevents David from future anxiety. Her plea to David is full of perception:

> The Lord will surely reward you with eternal royalty for your descendants, for you are fighting his battles; and you will never do wrong throughout your entire life. Even when you are chased by those who seek your life, you are safe in the care of the Lord your God, just as though you were safe inside his purse! But the lives of your enemies shall disappear like stones from a sling! When the Lord has done all the good things he promised you and has made you king of Israel, you won't want the conscience of a murderer who took the

> law into his own hands! And when the Lord has done
> these great things for you, please remember me!'
>
> (*1 Samuel 25:28 – 31,* The Living Bible)

When we are fighting the Lord's battles, we do not need to fight for ourselves. Anxiety-produced anger will only violate our consciences. Far better to leave God to work in the situation and simply to trust in him.

DISPROPORTIONATE FEAR

Anxiety then can take the form of a free-floating fear, apparently unconnected with any external stimulus. Or it may be a response to an event or a fear-provoking situation. This kind of anxiety is different from simple fear for two reasons: first, the fear becomes generalized — along with the initial fear-response comes a vague, uncertain sense of foreboding; second, in anxiety the fear is out of all proportion to the thing or event which produced it. The anxious person responds to situations in a different way from other people.

This kind of exaggerated fear-response can frequently be seen at work in church life. The 1960s saw the rise of the 'hippy' movement when many young people in Europe and America rejected the materialistic values of their parents. This generation, products of the New Deal or the Welfare State, began to feel that the way they had been brought up did not lead to personal satisfaction or fulfilment, so they adopted a free and easy lifestyle which gave birth to the teenage drug culture. Many young people became dropouts from society. Seeking something better, hordes of them experimented with hallucinatory drugs and Eastern mysticism. During this wide-scale questioning of values, some became disillusioned with their own revolt and began to re-examine the culture they had rejected. Out of this, came the 'Jesus People', a generation of youngsters who rejected the church but were fascinated by Jesus. Many of these young-sters were converted and eventually began to join conven-tional churches. The churches were rarely prepared for this strange invasion. Often, conventional church members became anxious at the appearance of bare-footed, ragged or bearded young worshippers. In some cases the anxiety reached fever-pitch and the newcomers were voted out of the church because of their outlandish manners and dress. Indeed, there were instances in which special 'hippy churches' had to be formed to accommodate the outcasts.

The anxiety which was expressed in the comments and attitudes of church members came from a fear of question-ing their own attitudes. The churches feared not so much for the dilution of their Christian faith, as for an imagined attack upon their predominantly middle-class sets of values.

GROUP DEFENCES

The Pharisees reacted in a similar way when Jesus preached to tax collectors and prostitutes, accepting them into the Kingdom of God. Group membership is often used as a defence against anxiety. Consequently, when the group is added to and changes in such a way as to threaten some of its central attitudes, anxiety breaks out and can result in extreme reactions.

The same thing can happen when the Spirit of God begins to move in an established group, or church, causing it to contemplate change. The Holy Spirit loves flexibility. He is a Spirit of change whose watchword is adaptability and he works this openness into the lives of those who truly know the Lord. Jesus himself commented to Nicodemus the Pharisee, 'The wind blows where it wishes, and you hear the sound of it, but cannot tell where it comes from and where it goes. So it is with everyone born of the Spirit' (John

3:8, RKJV). To follow where the Spirit leads is to be freed from anxiety. The trouble is that after an initial exhilarating encounter with him, we often retreat into rigidity. The known and tested are so much safer than a life of adventure with God the Holy Spirit. That is why we are so prone to hide behind formalism and tradition in our churches.

AN EXPLOSIVE EXPERIENCE

Charles, the chairman of the board of deacons in one church, was happy when a new pastor arrived. It relieved him of many anxious pressures. But soon his pleasure gave way to fear and eventually to anger. The new pastor's ministry was blessed by the arrival of several new Christians, but this blessing was accompanied by freer, unstructured worship. Charles was a man who operated by agenda, his bulwark lay in efficient administration. The new state of affairs caused him to feel threatened.

> *Charles could not cope, not because anything was wrong, but because of the way in which he had been brought up.*

Over the months, the level of Charles' anxiety rose, until one Sunday evening he walked out of the church building, shouting vengeance at the Pastor. His anxiety had boiled over into anger which he could no longer restrain. Later, he forced a showdown church meeting over certain issues. One thing he could not cope with was the spontaneous displays of affection between those Christians whose lives had been changed. Charles could not cope, not because anything was wrong, but because of the way in which he had been brought up.

As a child he had been taught that public displays of

affection were improper. Even as a baby his mother would not pick him up when he cried because the mother-care books of the period said it was not good for a child. Consequently, Charles had learned to fear positive emotion. The only public emotion displayed to him as a child was corrective. So he learned that it was safer to hide behind rules and that, in threatening situations, anger is an appropriate response. Both rule-keeping and anger stemmed from inbred anxiety. There are many Christians who share Charles' problem and their behaviour can make church an explosive experience for new believers.

ANXIETY FROM DEFEAT

The fear of defeat or failure often causes excessive anxiety. A biblical example can be seen when King Saul was confronted by Goliath. The Philistine champion was undoubtedly a formidable man, but his size and his armour are not sufficient grounds to explain Israel's response. Goliath demanded that the battle should be settled by individual combat. His threats were on a grand scale, 'I defy the armies of Israel this day; give me a man that we may fight together' (1 Samuel 17:10, AKJV). Perhaps it was the degree of Goliath's insolence that daunted Saul but we read, 'When Saul and all Israel heard these words of the Philistine, they were dismayed and greatly afraid.'

It is likely that the cause of Saul's dismay was the prospect of a public defeat, *on his own*. To die in battle with his whole army would somehow have been heroic. To suffer defeat alone in front of both sides defied contemplation. While Saul waited for someone else to conquer an enemy he was not prepared to face, he endured a daily parading of defeat. Each time the Philistine swaggered before the two armies, Saul's anxiety grew, and his sense of failure mounted. In the end he was prepared to let an untried youth — David — take on an enemy he could not accept for himself. The difference between David and Saul is clear. Saul remembered past disobediences before God and that the Spirit of the Lord had departed from him. The enemy had already won. David's confidence was in God. His assurance came from his past experience of God's deliverance and from his knowledge of God's character.

For many people the thought of failure gives rise to excessive anxiety. Usually this is based on a fear of looking foolish in front of others, and is often accompanied by a deep sense of shame at past failings. Secretly we feel that we have failed not only ourselves but the Lord. Furthermore, because we cannot forgive ourselves for our failures we tend to believe that God hasn't either. Even reminding ourselves of Bible verses such as 'I can do all things through Christ who strengthens me', only serves to increase our sense of condemnation. We cannot call upon the Lord because we are paralyzed by anxiety and fear.

MISPLACED ANXIETY

We have established, then, that misplaced anxiety is a fear-reaction. It may be caused directly by an external stimulus or it may appear to be without cause. In either case, the real source of the anxiety lies within the individual. At best, persistent anxiety results in a general sense of foreboding which dampens the enjoyment of living. At worst, it can have serious physical consequences. It is known that stress and anxiety are a contributory factor in the development of heart attacks. It has also been shown that anxiety aggravates and perhaps even causes some forms of arthritis. Some decades ago, hospital research demonstrated that the onset of both the common cold and cancer can be accelerated by as much as 300% when the patient is over-anxious.

There are occasions when mild anxiety can be productive, for it leads to action. However, excessive or misplaced anxiety paralyzes the will, so that the sufferer becomes incapable of rational thought or decisive conduct. Many Christians find that it is anxiety which robs them of the joy of their salvation and prevents victory over sin. Anxiety is a corrosive emotion, but if we can begin to understand it, we can begin to overcome it.

2

When Anxiety Becomes
a Problem

Some anxiety is healthy, when it is productive. In the New Testament the apostle Paul speaks of his daily 'anxiety' for all the churches (2 Corinthians 11:28). Other translations use 'deep concern' or 'the pressure of my concern'. This sense of concern is a facet of our love for people and our commitment to God's purposes. To show such concern is entirely proper, indeed it is an essential part of what it means for us to be 'in Christ'. However, concern can quickly turn into self-concern and from there it easily degenerates into anxiety. Self-love, left to itself, becomes anxiety.

HEALTHY ANXIETY

There is, then, a healthy and an unhealthy form of anxiety. For many Christians, even healthy anxiety can become a problem because they are so used to the other type that they can no longer tell the difference!

Jesus showed a healthy concern for his disciples. He took thought for their welfare and for their future development, spending time teaching them, even when the crowds were gone. He showed a similar concern for the multitudes, seeing them as 'sheep without a Shepherd', but he never allowed the concern to overwhelm him. It *moved* him to compassion, grief (as in the case of Lazarus) and indignation but it never *removed* him from his central concern to accomplish the will of his Father. Even on the one occasion when anxiety came near to deterring him in the garden of Gethsemane, he was still able to say, 'nevertheless, not my will, but yours, be done' (Luke 22:42, KJV). Jesus knew what it was to be anxious but not overwhelmed.

When Paul reminds husbands to 'love your wives' in Ephesians chapter five, he is talking about a concern between husband and wife which mirrors the redemptive love of Christ — 'as Christ loved the Church.' This is wholesome concern. Better never to let it degenerate into self-love; even within the marriage relationship that is simply lust. Unhealthy anxiety is a form of self-indulgence, healthy anxiety is, on the contrary, a signal to loving action.

This is neatly illustrated by the incident between the apostle Paul and Epaphroditus (Philippians 2:25 – 30). The Philippian Church sent Epaphroditus to comfort Paul in prison. Meantime Epaphroditus fell ill and after his recovery became concerned because word had been relayed to Philippi about his illness but not about the cure. These circumstances could easily have given rise to a destructive cycle of anxiety but Paul resolved the issue. 'I considered it necessary,' he said, 'to send to you Epaphroditus, my brother, fellow worker, and fellow soldier, but your messenger and the one who ministered to my need; since he was longing for you all, and was distressed because you had heard that he was sick. For indeed he was sick almost unto death, but God had mercy on him, and not only on him but on me also, lest I should have sorrow upon sorrow.

Therefore I sent him the more eagerly, that when you see him again you may rejoice, and I may be less sorrowful.'

Paul's healthy concern led him to a course of action which relieved the potentially unhealthy anxiety generated both in Epaphroditus and in his 'brothers and sisters' at Philippi!

> **Unhealthy anxiety is a form of self-indulgence, healthy anxiety is, on the contrary, a signal to loving action.**

Another example of healthy anxiety occurs in the life of Paul during the shipwreck described in Acts, chapter 27. Paul had received a vision during the night that everyone would survive. In consequence he said '...take heart, men, for I believe God that it will be just as he told me' (Acts 27:25, RKJV). But he went on to say, 'However, we must run aground on a certain island' (Acts 27:26), and throughout the ensuing action Paul was anxious for his instructions to be followed. Being assured of God's purposes is not opposed to a healthy anxiety, because healthy anxiety creates growth.

UNHEALTHY ANXIETY

By contrast, unhealthy anxiety results either in a paralysis of the will or in inappropriate action. How often have you been stuck in a traffic queue at a junction behind a hesitant, anxious driver? All too frequently they hesitate to pull out when there are well-defined gaps in the stream of traffic on the main road. Before too long you and the other drivers behind you build up a dangerous level of impatience. Then, suddenly, when the stream of traffic flowing across you is densest and most dangerous, the anxious driver pulls out, almost causing an accident. Anxiety had begun by paralyz-ing the driver's will. He was unable to make a working deci-sion. Gradually, the anxiety level mounted, and when it became intolerable, he took impulsive action totally inappropriate to the circumstances.

Paralysis of the will

This often afflicts anxious people. The biblical example of David's behaviour when he fled from the anger of King Saul illustrates what we mean. We read in 1 Samuel, chapter 21 verse 10, that David took refuge in Gath, placing himself under the protection of the Philistine ruler, Achish. The ser-vants of King Achish pointed out to him David's reputation in Israel as a warrior. Immediately David discerned that his presence could be interpreted by his host as a threat. Then we read a surprising statement about the man who had taken on the champion of the Philistine army alone, 'Now David took these words to heart and was very much afraid of Achish the King of Gath' (1 Samuel 21:12, RKJV).

Not knowing whether to stay or flee, David acted the part of a madman. Anxiety kept him from making a clear deci-sion and eventually led him into double-dealing and sub-terfuge. The man who once fearlessly relied upon the Lord was reduced to living on his own wits by lying. Failure to be decisive put David at the mercy of someone else's deci-sion. Anxiety kept him from referring the matter to God. The church today encounters a similar paralysis of the will when it is all too anxious about what the world may think of the way it behaves.

Anxiety frequently results in the inability to make deci-sions. For the Christian it often leads to an unwillingness to trust the Lord. What begins as concern ends in a constant state of worry. The longer we worry at the problem, approaching it from all sides, up and down, the more difficult it becomes to decide anything. Drawbacks become insurmountable barriers and the more we ponder the less we are able to come to a conclusion.

Anxiety and the healthy

Anxiety can also attack even the most robust personality, leading to a feeling of helplessness and moral paralysis. Such an event is recorded in the life of the great English Baptist preacher of the nineteenth century, Charles Haddon Spurgeon. His career as a young preacher was so successful in terms of attracting crowds that he and his deacons hired the Music Hall in the Royal Surrey Gardens in London to accommodate the evening congregation. This novel procedure attracted so much comment from the press that the hall could not accommodate the crowds who turned out to the first service held there.

During the service, while Spurgeon was leading in prayer, a group of mischief-makers who had placed themselves in different parts of the building began to shout 'Fire'. Many of the audience panicked and rushed for the exits. Seeing that there was no evidence of a fire, Spurgeon grasped the situation and attempted to calm the crowd. In order to achieve this he was advised to begin preaching, which he did. Unknown to the platform party, however, the balustrade on an external staircase had collapsed. Seven people were trampled to death and twenty-eight were severely injured.

When Spurgeon eventually realized what had happened, he was devastated. It took him two weeks to recover from the shock sufficiently to begin preaching again. The Church Minute Book covering the period records, 'This lamentable circumstance produced very serious effects on the nervous system of our Pastor. He was entirely prostrated for some days, and compelled to relinquish his preaching engagements. Through the great mercy of our Heavenly Father, he was, however, restored so as to be able to occupy the pulpit in our own Chapel on Sunday, November 2nd, and gradually recovered his wonted health and vigour.'

The great preacher's will was paralyzed for several days. He was brought low by anguish and grief. All of this fed his anxiety about public attitudes towards the Lord and his church, not to mention his own reputation. A deluge of thoughts rushed through his mind, reducing him to a state of inaction and physical weakness.

Writing a year after the event, Spurgeon recalled the events of that terrible evening and the days which followed: 'When, like a whirlwind, the destruction was overpast, when the whole of its devastation was visible to my eyes, who can conceive the anguish of my sad spirit? I refused to be comforted; tears were my meat by day, and dreams my terror by night. I felt as I had never felt before...Then came the 'slander of many' — barefaced fabrications, libellous insinuations, and barbarous accusations. These alone might have scooped out the last drop of consolation from my cup of happiness; but the worst had come to the worst, and the utmost malice of the enemy could do no more. Lower they cannot sink who are already in the nethermost depths.' For a few days Spurgeon was unable to bring himself to read his Bible, to pray or to make decisions.

Fortunately, Spurgeon did not totally lose his grasp of faith in God and in the midst of his anxiety, his sense of proportion was restored to him. He reports, 'On a sudden, like a flash of lightning from the sky, my soul returned to me. The burning lava of my brain cooled in an instant. The throbbings of my brow were still, the cool wind of comfort fanned my cheek, which had been scorched in the furnace...On wings of a dove my spirit mounted to the stars — yea, beyond them. Whither did it wing its flight, and where did it sing its song of gratitude? It was at the feet of Jesus, whose name charmed its fears, and placed an end to its mourning.'

Spurgeon describes this event, which took place in the garden of his home, as like a second conversion experience. 'I was a man again,' he says, 'and what is more, a believer. The garden in which I stood became an Eden to me and the spot was most solemnly consecrated in my restored consciousness...Never since the day of my conversion had I known so much of this infinite excellence, never had my spirit leaped with such unutterable delight.'

The expression of this experience may be that of a more fulsome age but it graphically portrays the reality of what the man went through. A lesser man may have cracked, permanently losing his hold on God, for anxiety kills faith. As it was, he came near to letting go. No wonder that when he later founded his college for training pastors, Spurgeon took as its motto 'Teneo ut teneor' — 'I both grasp and am grasped'. Faith rescued him from the immediate effects of anxiety.

Fortunately, Spurgeon did not totally lose his grasp of faith in God and in the midst of his anxiety, his sense of proportion was restored to him.

Nevertheless, an underlying strain of anxiety relating to this event never left Spurgeon. Shindler, in his *Life and Labours of Pastor C. H. Spurgeon* tells how, twenty-five years later, a disturbance in the crowd at the Baptist Union open session in Portsmouth, affected Spurgeon.

'Long before the service began, every available seat and all standing room were occupied, and still there were hundreds pressing forward and endeavouring to crowd in. There was some confusion just as the preacher was passing on to the platform to take his seat. He seemed entirely unmanned, and stood in the passage leaning his head on his hand. He told the writer that the circumstances so vividly recalled the scene at the Surrey Music Hall, that he felt quite unable to preach. But he did preach, and preach well, though he could not entirely recover from the agitation of his nervous system.'

Another colleague, Pastor W. Williams, relates in his *Personal Reminiscences of Charles Haddon Spurgeon* how the mere quotations of the text from which he had planned to speak on the night of the disaster, caused Spurgeon dismay. Williams comments, 'I cannot but think, from what I then saw, that his comparative early death might be in some measure due to the furnace of mental affliction he endured on and after that fearful night.'

Even when the immediate effects of anxiety are dealt with, experiences can lay down an underlying strand of anxiety which re-emerges from time to time. This, together with other symptoms of anxiety, will be examined later. However, Spurgeon's experience in which his will-power was temporarily paralyzed, draws attention to the fact that there are a number of associated or related emotions to which anxiety attaches itself. Such feelings as grief, guilt, remorse, fear and helplessness often give rise to anxiety and, in turn, feed off it.

Inappropriate responses

When anxiety does not lead to a paralysis of the will, it usually leads to inappropriate action. As we saw earlier, in the case of the hesitant driver, it sometimes results in both responses successively. By inappropriate action we mean actions which are not warranted by the circumstances.

This kind of anxiety response is likely to occur where the situation provokes an emotional response out of proportion to the event or the threat produced by it. The real problem is an internal one. Over-reaction arises from a pre-disposition to anxiety. This pre-disposition itself generally arises out of past experiences.

Just such an example can be seen in the life of King Herod in the New Testament. When the Magi arrived in Jerusalem heralding the birth of Jesus, they naturally enquired at the palace 'where is he who has been born King of the Jews?' We read, 'When Herod heard these things he was troubled, and all Jerusalem with him.'

Herod's anxiety caused him to call together the religious leaders to find out where the Messiah was to be born. Clearly, he understood that the birth which had been predicted was not that of an ordinary earthly king. Although Herod was an Idumean and not a Jew, he was sufficiently conversant with Jewish customs and with the Old Testament to be aware of God's intentions for the nation in the form of a deliverer — Messiah. When he elicited the answer to his questions, Herod took deceptive steps to find the child, Jesus. As soon as it became clear to him that the visiting wise men had avoided him on their return journey, Herod put out the order to slaughter all of the male infants under the age of two in Bethlehem.

> *Over-reaction arises from a pre-disposition to anxiety. This pre-disposition itself generally arises out of past experiences.*

This extreme response was no doubt born of heightened anxiety. If Herod had been a just and legally installed ruler, he had nothing to fear from the Messiah. But his conscience was troubled, and his anxiety fuelled, by the fact that he was, in reality, a puppet-King who had managed to persuade the Romans to install him to the throne in spite of the fact that he wasn't even a Jew. Moreover, Herod had maintained his position as king by ruthless suppression even of members of his own family. History records that he was so fearful of intrigue and palace coups that he poisoned his own wife.

The unjust means by which he had gained the throne kept Herod riddled with anxiety lest someone else might succeed in doing the same to him. Consequently, his efforts to secure his position became more and more extreme, less and less appropriate. His current anxiety was born in his past experience. This is the way in which many of us handle anxiety.

To take a more recent example: Howard Hughes, the multi-millionaire recluse, locked himself away from the rest of the world because he feared infection. During the last few years of his life he would see no one face to face. He preferred to use a sanitized telephone. His meals were served by staff wearing gloves. In the end, his whole life became an elaborate ritual of disinfecting objects and avoiding personal contact. Apparently he became obsessively afraid of contracting some infectious disease which might kill him. His anxiety reached such a pitch that, in spite of his millions, his quality of life was miserable. Many Christians behave in this way within the church. They are so afraid of being hurt if they are open to others that they shut themselves off from anything more than formal contacts with other believers. Sitting on a rich pile of God's fellowship-treasures, they live like spiritual recluses. Afraid of catching anything bad, they fail to contract anything that is good. Anxiety and mistrust are constant bed-fellows.

Causes

Unhealthy anxiety, then, may appear to be uncaused. Alternatively, the immediate cause may be obvious but the response to it exaggerated. In either case, the cause is to be found at a deeper level. We may not see the cause but it is always there. An anxious personality is usually the result of past experiences. There are rare instances where chronic anxiety is caused by a chemical imbalance in the brain. However, the most common causes of it are to be found deep down within the personality. In the next two chapters we are going to look at the characteristics of anxious people and then at the characteristics of anxious congregations. For churches, as well as individuals, can become anxiety-ridden.

PART

2

DYNAMICS

How Anxiety Works

3

The Anxious Individual

I n this chapter we are going to discuss some of the leading characteristics of the anxious person. We will begin
by isolating these characteristics and then proceed to
illustrate some typical clusters of behaviour related to anxiety. The illustrations will be taken from actual case studies,
although the names and occasionally some of the details,
have been changed to protect anonymity.

PROFILE OF THE ANXIOUS PERSON

Very seldom will one anxious individual present all the
characteristics which follow. Nevertheless, they are, individually, typical manifestations of anxiety. In practice, they
will tend to occur in clusters constituting individual behaviour patterns. These clusters of behaviour may be referred
to as an 'anxiety syndrome'.

• **Tense.** The anxious person is often worried, not by
specific events which have already happened, but by things
which he imagines *may* happen. Rather than living in the
reality of the present, anxious people tend to live in fear of

the future. This apprehensiveness gives rise to a tense personality. Those near to him are well aware of the tension experienced by the anxious person. This tension will often be clearly signalled by bodily posture. It can manifest itself in taut facial muscles, frequently accompanied by rigid back and neck muscles, causing tense headaches and even migraine.

• **Irritable.** A constant state of tension causes irritability. Physical tension and emotional tension brought about by anxiety compounds the initial problem. This build-up and reinforcement of emotional and physical tension tends to surface in irritability. Frequently, when we are irritable with others, it is because we are irritated with ourselves. The root cause is usually anxiety, reinforced by a sense of inadequacy and guilt. Christians in particular are liable to feel guilty because they realize their anxiety is a denial of the caring purposes of God.

• **Angry.** Anger is one stop further down the anxiety-line. Irritability can, to some extent, be hidden or suppressed. The trouble is that any suppressed emotion merely goes underground, and a sufficiently jarring experience causes that irritability to erupt into anger. We may have hidden the tension and irritability but eventually we will either give vent to it in the form of anger or it will lead to emotional illness. Anxiety and aggression are spiritually not far apart.

• **Intimidated.** Anxiety often causes the sufferer to feel intimidated by life. Something in particular may provoke the anxiety, but once it has been aroused it tends to become generalized. A haunting sense of unease or non-specific foreboding will grip the person's mind, sometimes accompanied by a vague feeling of having forgotten to do something important. Or there may be a feeling that past actions might lead to dire consequences in the future. Life seems to be capricious and threatening. The result is an intimidated, cowed, personality.

• **Restless.** A general restlessness frequently accompanies a sense of intimidation. Because the anxious person cannot feel confident of the outcome of any of life's events, he finds it difficult to settle to a definite course of conduct. Uncertainty about the future results in an unwillingness to make current commitments. This kind of restlessness is close to a lack of faith in the goodness of God and is often based in the lack of a sense of self-worth.

• **Indecisive.** Restless anxiety can often lead to indecisive conduct. Because he has a sense of foreboding about the outcome of any action, the chronically anxious person finds it difficult to make up his mind. Uncertainty and fear about what might happen, leads to hesitance. Often this hesitation arises out of a fear of making mistakes.

• **Ritualistic.** Another way of coping with indecision is to retreat into ritualism. An intimidated and indecisive person will often play safe by sticking to known patterns of behaviour. He will become a creature of habit, fearful of launching out into uncharted waters. The safest way to handle uncertainty and indecision is to stay with a tested routine. The resultant lifestyle may be humdrum but is relatively certain. such a person may become so trapped by habitual behaviour that any change of routine becomes a threat, and in order to avoid such changes the sufferer will tend to protect himself behind a wall of ritualistic behaviour. This is the kind of person who checks the contents of his pockets three times before leaving the house. He will also bolt, bar and padlock the door, making sure he takes exactly the same route to catch the bus. Such rituals, which go beyond reason, are designed to allay anxiety by producing a sense of security in the known and tested.

• **Over-cautious.** The anxiously indecisive person will, over a period of time, become over-cautious in his attitude to life in general. The inability to be decisive about specific large-scale issues gradually becomes translated into a pervasive attitude. The agonies of decision-making can often be seen on such a person's face. They will tend to allow other people to make decisions for them. The same over-cautious person will bottle up his anxiety until, paradoxically, it breaks out in reckless actions.

• **Over-protective.** When an anxious person is responsible for someone else, they tend to be excessively protective. So it is that parents can breed anxiety within their children, and a cycle of behaviour is set up which is passed on from generation to generation.

• **Approval seeking.** A further consequence of over-protectiveness for the child is that it will indulge in excessive approval-seeking. A child who always wants to impress the teacher, for instance, is often seeking to be reassured that it is accepted. The approval-seeking behaviour is usually born of parental anxiety which causes the child to feel insecure.

When excessive approval-seeking persists into adult life it can lead to adults filling the wrong job. Some preachers, for example, find their fulfilment in the plaudits of people rather than the appreciation of God. So they tell people what they think they want to hear rather than what they need to know. This can be because they are perpetuating infantile patterns of approval-seeking.

These then are some of the common symptoms of anxiety. They will rarely occur all together in one person's behaviour, but they do tend to occur in clusters. The following case studies, taken from real life, will illustrate the ways in which typical clusters can develop.

TENSION, IRRITABILITY AND EXPLOSIVE ANGER

When Jack and Helen came into the counselling room, their marriage was on the verge of collapse. He was an airline pilot, she a housewife. Apparent tension and irritability flowed from every word they spoke, revealing their inability to communicate with each other. Words poured out but there was no communication. Both of them looked tense and each tended to snap at, or contradict, the other.

Jack was seldom at home owing to the nature of his job. When rostering permitted him to come home, his own projects interested him more than the family. Helen, meantime, had taken refuge in a social life which consumed all her activities. Both Jack and Helen's church commitment was of a shallow and legalistic nature. They belonged to an evangelical church where the emphasis was upon conforming to a set of religious rules. Consequently, appearances were more important than cultivating openness and reality. Their personal relationship with Jesus was even more shallow and discussion of this caused embarrassment, leading to greater tension and irritability.

Helen had been consistently unfaithful to her husband. She resented his long absences and his lack of attention to her. When Jack confronted her with her unfaithfulness, in the counselling room, she did not deny it but exploded, passing the blame back to him.

The tension, irritability and anger which were evident in the counselling situation were based on ignorance and misconceptions which, in turn, had given rise to acute anxiety. Since the beginning of their marriage the couple had never communicated with each other what they expected of marriage or each other. Neither had they verbalized what they expected of each other in their relationship with the Lord.

During conversation, Helen would explode if words were not used accurately. She would painstakingly stop and correct any slight misuse of language. This gave a clue to what underlay her attitudes. Helen was aware of the least violation of legal standards. Her whole attitude to life was governed by the letter rather than the spirit of the law and she used this as a defensive weapon. Little wonder that she had no experience of the freedom of the Holy Spirit in her life.

It turned out that Jack and Helen had engaged in premarital sex. This had given rise to a sense of guilt. Because it entailed a violation of their legalistic outlook, Jack and Helen were not able to deal with their failure and find forgiveness. This had brought about a double consequence: first, they had buried the guilt, thus preventing them from communicating with each other about love; second, the sense of defilement at their promiscuity had led to an anxious belief that sex was dirty. As a result they could not express love within the marriage.

Jack found consolation in his work and in his private interests. Nevertheless, this left him tense and irritable and increasingly suspicious of Helen's activities. This anxious suspicion more and more frequently broke out in displays of anger.

Helen, in turn, felt neglected as a result of Jack's conduct. Since she regarded sexual activity as dirty, she could not express her affection to her husband. She turned increasingly to illicit sexual affairs which she excused as revenge upon Jack.

Meantime, her sense of guilt increased as did her anxiety at being found out. As she saw Jack as the initiator of the original promiscuity, her anxiety fused into a smouldering anger against him. He was to blame. Whenever it seemed likely she would be found out by him, Helen would pick fault with his words, flying into a rage.

Fortunately, the counsellor was able to confront Jack and Helen with their anxieties and the root of their behaviour. they both made a deep commitment to the Lord Jesus, in the counselling room. Forgiveness was administered and abso-lution, in the name of Christ, dealt with their anxiety.

Now Jack and Helen are happily married and have helped many others to a fuller marriage experience. Needless to say, they are committed, Spirit filled workers in their local Church. They still have periodic problems but they have learned to deal with anxiety by taking it to the Lord and seeking his forgiveness and a new start.

INDECISIVE, PLAY SAFE, OVER-RECKLESS

Gwyn remembers when he was a child he would sometimes postpone a difficult decision by saying to himself, 'If the next car to come along is red, I will turn left at the bottom of the street. If it isn't, I will turn right!' Children often make a decision depending on whether they step on a crack in the pavement or upon the toss of a coin. All of these are devices to take the responsibility for decision-making out of their own hands.

All too often, adults continue this childish pattern of behaviour. It is an artificial way of coping with the indeci-siveness produced by anxiety. Unfortunately, many Christians treat prayer in this way. They tend to make guid-ance depend on a set of events which are apparently out-side of their control. Although this may occasionally be permissible, this approach to guidance means that the adult is shirking his responsibility. At worst, it can be a way of blaming God for decisions which anxiety makes difficult.

Jean Brown was reckless in her choice of a marriage partner. She knew that Earl was attracted to her and was likely to propose. In spite of his obvious unsuitability — he was jealous and tended to be violent — Jean let the decision depend upon circumstances. She told herself that if Earl were to propose to her within a particular time and in a particular way, she would agree. The conditions were met and eventually they married. The marriage turned out to be disastrous and ended in divorce.

Subsequently Jean became a Christian but she did not give up her indecisive behaviour. She had a good job which was interesting and reasonably well paid. However, in the course of the marital break-up, she lost her home and ended up in a bedsit. Jean would bemoan her fate, particularly to her married Christian friends. She could never understand the problems *they* were encountering. She could only see the disadvantages of her own situation. Increasingly she became a creature of habit. She longed for a new Christian partner but, apart from attending worship, she never went where she might meet someone suitable. Jean became cautious about friendships, taking care to speak to few people even at work.

Jean received the impression that most of her decisions were wrong. She was given little encouragement by mother or father.

Jean found her bedsit uncomfortable, expensive and situated too far from her church and a potential circle of Christian friends. She constantly complained about this but when alternative suggestions were made, she was always evasive. Eventually, her church established some single person's flats for rent, in order to bring people like Jean together. Her name was high on the list of those who would benefit.

She was approached by the church leaders and shown over a flat. Suddenly Jean found as many reasons why her existing bedsit was suitable as she had previously given for its inconvenience! Jean could not make up her mind; to make decisions only increased her level of anxiety. She had learned to cope with existing anxieties by ritualistic behaviour which included ritual complaints about a situation she was not prepared to alter.

Closer investigation revealed that Jean's anxiety about making decisions went back to her childhood. Her younger brother was disabled by cerebral palsy and her mother was constantly unwell. Her father could not help much in the home, owing to the nature of his work. Consequently Jean was forced to take on an adult role very early in life. Before she was twelve she was required to make responsible decisions about family expenditure which were beyond her years. Because she was unwell, Jean's mother was often irritable. Consequently Jean received the impression that most of her decisions were wrong. She was given little encouragement by mother or father.

From these beginnings, her anxiety had developed and she often avoided making decision by letting events take over. When she had sometimes delayed a decision too long, Jean would feel forced to act suddenly. Often these last-minute decisions would go wrong, thus causing more anxiety.

It was in these circumstances that Jean learned to hide behind procedures which were calculated to avoid having to make up her mind. This led to her disastrous marriage and her subsequent retreat within herself. Now, with the help of Christian friends, she is painfully learning the discipline of freedom in the Lord. It will take her some time to learn to deal with her anxiety and become her authentic self once more.

ATTENTION-SEEKING, OVER-PROTECTIVE

Don Keane was a World War II baby. After his conception his father did not return until the war had ended. His mother was over-protective towards him. He was her only child and, as far as she knew, her husband might never return from the war. In consequence, Mrs Keane alternated between over-indulging Don and making excessive demands upon him. Most of these demands were designed for his protection. Hence, Don was not allowed to play out with the other children and it was always impressed upon the boy to stay near to his mother.

When Don's father returned from the army, his presence became an additional source of anxiety. Here was someone who competed for his mother's attention. Don began to make self-indulgent demands on his mother and, when it appeared that his father was receiving more attention, he would throw a tantrum. If this did not work he would strive to excel in order to impress his father. Occasionally, his anger would be physically vented upon Mrs Keane.

Don's father rarely corrected him. Possibly he felt that the boy had been sufficiently deprived during the war years. Instead, he over-indulged his son and whenever Don got into difficulties his father would come to his rescue, even when correction would have been a more appropriate response. During his teenage period, Don made a public profession of faith in Christ. However, his commitment was shallow and unreal. He viewed God as an indulgent father who would bale him out of difficulties whenever he panicked into prayer. Well into adult life, his natural father would still have to buy him out of frequent financial scrapes.

Don's attitude to church life mirrored his family experience. He loved to be in the place of prominence and would ask to preach whenever he could. He was good with words and could make an impression, briefly. However, when more responsibility followed his show of ability, Don would cave in. His anxiety about keeping up his 'ministry' would cause him to withdraw, only to join up with another church. Here the whole pattern would be repeated. In each case, Don would fly to the Pastor of the church for protection, always coming up with plausible reasons for his failure. Usually it was held to be someone else's fault.

In his late forties he still behaves like a spoiled child, alternately throwing tantrums and switching on the charm.

Don was always competing for attention. His two marriages failed because neither wife was able to protect him the way his mother did. Furthermore, his anxiety and frustration at marital responsibility, which he could not carry, was vented in physical violence towards his marriage partners. Even now, Don has not been able to come to terms with his anxieties about acceptance. In his mid fifties he still behaves like a spoiled child, alternately throwing tantrums and switching on the charm.

Over-protectiveness builds anxiety into a child partly because it too stems from anxiety. A recent newspaper report carried the story of some wayward boys who broke into a house in their own neighbourhood. When they forced entry, they discovered a little girl locked in the room of whom nobody in the area was aware. She was not materially deprived, the room contained the best of everything.

Her mother was simply afraid that if the child went out to play, she might be hurt. Instead, untold emotional damage was inflicted. It is highly likely that this little girl will herself grow into an anxious, over-protective adult.

ANXIETY REACTIONS

In its more extreme forms, anxiety can result in physical illness. Alternatively, it can give rise to severe temporary manifestations such as breathlessness, palpitations or even temporary paralysis.

Mildred Powers is an attractive and capable young woman. She has a career, an outgoing personality and is a natural leader who has been used to working with teenagers. Nevertheless, for a time, she suffered from anxiety reactions. Frequently, when Mildred was in a prayer meeting, she would panic and feel like running away. The same symptoms would occur in any situation where she might be expected to speak to a group. As time went on the reaction became more severe and Mildred would fight for breath. Once or twice she passed out with asthmatic symptoms. There was no history of asthma in her family and her doctor rejected this as a diagnosis.

Eventually, Mildred came for counselling and in the course of ministry it was discovered that she was subconsciously fighting grief over past hurts. Over the years, Mildred had been let down by a number of people who were close to her. When she was young her grandparents died suddenly. They were very close to her and, irrationally, she felt rejected. Moreover, her parents strongly discouraged any display of grief which she bottled up. Consequently, over a period of years, Mildred learned to hide grief, tension or hurts, so when she found herself in a healthily tense situation she would begin to panic. Particularly when Mildred felt that other eyes would be upon her, watching her reaction, the suppressed sense of rejection would surface. The panic manifested itself in asthmatic symptoms.

Once this was discovered, counsellors prayed with Mildred for emotional healing. The Lord graciously met her in her need and gave her release in her spirit. Within three days she was able to stand up in a full church meeting and testify without any physical symptoms. Occasionally the fears have returned but Mildred has learned to rebuke them in the name of the Lord. She has discovered that they are a ploy of the enemy to cause her to feel rejected. Now she has learned to cope with the grief of disappointment and is entering a new phase of usefulness to the Lord.

CAUSES OF ANXIETY

A common feature of these case-studies is that the anxiety goes back to earlier events. Decisions which were made, or experiences which were entered upon, earlier in life began a chain of anxious behaviour. In most cases the anxiety which found expression was not appropriate to the events which triggered them off.

> *To be permanently, or even frequently, vaguely fearful, is to deny the love of God for us.*

Many people become over-anxious in the face of relatively trivial situations. Sometimes far more potentially threatening events will leave the same person unmoved. The particular type of event acts as a trigger to anxiety, just as certain foods may trigger off physical allergies. Usually the anxiety-promoting situation is in some way similar to the events which began the anxiety pattern. For instance,

Mildred Powers feared her ability to hide her emotions when called upon to perform in public. Because of past experience, she sub-consciously judged that her possible failure to handle her emotions would cause people to reject her. The chain of anxious behaviour which led to such extreme symptoms began in childhood. It was there that she first began to assume that being accepted depended on controlling or suppressing her emotions. But that act of self-control itself heightened her anxiety!

A similar sort of mechanism operates in most cases of over-anxious behaviour. This knowledge does not excuse our behaviour. It simply helps us to understand what we are doing. It is not in God's nature to want us to hang on to anxiety. For to be permanently, or even frequently, vaguely fearful, is to deny the love of God for us. 'Cast all your cares upon Him for he cares for you' it says in 1 Peter, chapter 5, verse 7. There is both biblical and linguistic justification for translating this verse, 'Casting all your *anxieties* upon Him, for He is *anxious* for you!' The word 'to cast' is also important. As someone has said, 'you cannot cast a stone unless you first let it go.' The same principle applies to individual anxieties.

One of the issues we have to confront is that where there are chronically anxious people, an atmosphere of anxiety builds up. As a consequence, it is possible for 'corporate anxiety' to be a real factor in our human behaviour, and for churches as well as individuals to become anxious.

4

The Anxious Congregation

Anxiety is a contagious disease. Congregations as well as individuals can be motivated by anxious feelings. If there are enough anxious people within a given group of individuals, the group itself will tend to display some of the attributes of anxiety. Let us remind ourselves of our working definition of anxiety: 'Anxiety is a fear reaction from within. No outside stimulus is necessary. The term is used to represent a displeasurable response which is out of proportion to the fear-producing situation.'

Plainly, a congregation is capable of a fear reaction which comes from within. It is equally possible that such a fear-response may come without any external stimulus or, alternatively, it may be an exaggerated response to events which are taking place outside of that congregation.

LESSONS FROM HISTORY

Arthur Miller's play, *The Crucible*, deals with events which occurred in a community in Massachusetts in its early days as a colony. The Puritan Church which formed the community was isolated and inbred. The demands of self-discipline and self-examination which were made on it by the Pastor were severe. A group of children, mainly girls, caught in a childish misdemeanour in the woods began to accuse one another of secret practices. It seemed a good way of explaining away their responsibility. The adult section of the community were scandalized. The girls were brought to trial and the prosecutor's morbid questioning about the children's fantasies caused one of them to be convinced she had been dealing with the devil. The anxiety of the adult community rose. Faced with its own repressed guilt feelings, a scapegoat became necessary to the community. One of its number was found guilty of witchcraft and was executed.

Miller used a historical case as a guise to attack the McCarthyite anti-communist witch-hunts of the 1950s in the United States. In both cases (the Salem Witch trials and the excesses of the McCarthy era) corporate hysteria was fuelled by anxiety. These may be fairly extreme cases, but corporate anxiety is not an uncommon phenomenon.

LOSS OF CONTROL

A church in southern Britain was dominated by a wealthy individual. A prominent member of the congregation and a deacon, he owned a large business which employed other members of the church. The congregation had a reputation for breaking ministers. Pastor after pastor left in fairly rapid succession. Whenever a fresh incumbent began to establish himself and show any strength of character and leadership he would either be squeezed out or voted from his post. It seemed that the businessman on the diaconate could not cope with anyone who might be as strong as himself. Firm leadership posed a threat to his security. He was the boss at work and he meant to be the boss in the church.

As soon as this businessman was confronted with an

independently-minded pastor, his anxiety rose. People around him in the church depended upon him financially and psychologically. After all, he had remained in the saddle through a succession of ministers. He represented stability and security. A differing viewpoint on the part of the pastor represented emotional and organizational upheaval. It was little wonder that the congregations anxiety rose in relation to that of the businessman. Ministers stood little chance of survival in the face of such corporate anxiety. But what characterizes such an anxious congregation?

PROFILE OF THE ANXIOUS CONGREGATION

Just as with the anxious individual, it is possible to construct a profile of the anxious congregation. The list of 'symptoms' which will rarely take place all at once in any one church, but will often occur individually in congregations. Once several of them are found together, the congregation is heading for trouble. It has become an anxious congregation.

• **Restless insecurity.** A church, as a body of people, may fall into restlessness and insecurity. It will often be difficult to pinpoint the source, or even the nature, of this restlessness. However, criticism is usually a feature of the restless congregation. Fired by insecurity about where they are going (or perhaps about where someone is trying to take them) the members of such a church will tend to criticize their leaders.

Criticism will not be confined to decisions and the way they are made. It will also extend to other members of the group. Frequently, leaders will be accused of manipulation and cliques will form, giving rise to divisiveness and further criticism. Every fresh initiative tends to be greeted with suspicion. This leads, in turn, to an increase in restlessness and every new suggestion becomes a threat to the congregational security.

Churches exercising a congregational form of government are especially prone to such anxious restlessness. In such circumstances the process of voting often leads to an unedifying adoption of political processes. Instead of seeking the mind of the Lord, power blocks start to form around issues, and factions emerge. Soon, canvassing and lobbying for support sets in before the church meeting takes place. All this only serves to increase the sense of insecurity which led to the initial restless atmosphere of the church.

• **Inability to decide.** Congregations displaying anxious restlessness develop a chronic inability to make decisions. The leaders feel unsupported and unwilling to decide upon issues. The congregation itself cannot make decisions because they are only presented with weak and divided recommendations. Every decision point becomes a debate, each issue turns into an argument and the church gives in to bickering instead of going forward in faith.

Even when decisions are made in such a context, individuals, and even groups, within the congregation will refuse to implement them. Anxiety over the motives of their opponents causes them to reject decisions that have been made. The congregation will then become subversive. Satan has a field-day reducing what was meant to be a decisive and prophetic community into a dithering spiritual jelly!

• **Undefined caution.** An indecisive congregation will often display an undefined caution. Though it is right to 'test the spirits, whether they are of God' (1 John 4:1, RKJV), this is not the caution of testing with a view to assessing and, if possible, adopting a course of action. Rather it is the caution born of rejection.

It is often felt better to dismiss a new course of action out of hand than to consider moving on. This may be because the tried and tested can be more comfortable than the unknown. It ignores the fact that standing still can result in stagnation.

• **Fear of making mistakes.** A major reason for undefined caution in a local congregation may be the fear of making mistakes. Whenever a major decision has to be made in such a congregation, the level of anxiety rises sharply. Perhaps past experiences of making mistakes will contribute to this sense of anxiety. Sometimes the cause is rooted in a wrong view of God. A congregation which fears the Lord and is concerned to do his will may actually be afraid to make a decision in case it is the wrong one. It may be felt that once they step out of the Lord's will, it is impossible to get back in line with him again. This is based on the implicit view that God is waiting to pounce on our mistakes and chastise us for them. It ignores the fact that God judges our desires as much as our actions. It also overlooks the fact that we can just as easily step out of God's will by failing to make a decision as we can by making the wrong one. Quite simply, not to make a decision can be the wrong decision!

We can fail God by inaction just as much as by rash or precipitate action. A fine balance needs to be kept between the extremes of presumption and stubbornness. Both are roundly condemned in Scripture. Fear of making mistakes is a paralyzing form of anxiety in any group of people.

• **Unwilling to accept reality.** A further consequence of anxiety in the congregation can be an unwillingness to accept reality. Thus many a church, living on in the cosy after-glow of the past, fails to realize that events have moved on. Such a church will fail to recognize dwindling congregations or the lack of the presence of God in worship. Rather, it will assume that things are as they should be and, when the decline is pointed out, will rationalize it in some way.

There are many ways in which whole congregations refuse to face up to reality. Usually this is because to do so would mean to contemplate change. It is this thought which creates anxiety: change means discomfort; to depart from the tried and tested risks an unexpected outcome. This risk cannot be confronted because, for most people, uncertainty breeds anxious doubts. The easiest solution is for the congregation to behave like a corporate ostrich, burying its head in the sand, hoping the threat will go away.

• **Irritable atmosphere.** An anxiety-ridden congregation will often generate an irritable atmosphere. Whatever the cause of the anxiety may be, once it is unleashed it tends to put people 'on edge'. Members of the anxious congregation tend to be suspicious of the motives of others. Whenever a suggestion is made or a change is contemplated, the members eye one another, looking for the advantage. What should be a brotherhood, based on mutual trust, can rapidly become more like a spy-ring! Suspicion of the motives of other Christians in the Body of Christ is probably one of the most frequent causes of back-biting and slander.

What should be a brotherhood, based on mutual trust, can rapidly become more like a spy-ring!

In the New Testament, the Apostle Paul addressed himself to the problem at least as frequently as he did to the ostensibly more major problems of sexual immorality. The reason is plain. Sexual immorality is a sin against one's own body. Criticism and slander is a sin against the Body of Christ. It leads to distrust, division and corporate impotence. Anxiety about the motives of other Christians builds up an irritable and potentially explosive atmosphere.

Just as individual anxiety can lead to physical illness, so corporate anxiety makes Christ's Body on earth sick. The Apostle Paul points to this possibility when he speaks to the Corinthian church about their competitive attitude to the Lord's Supper. Anxiety on the part of some members lest others should benefit from their contribution of food to the love-feast meant that they failed to discern the true nature of the church as the Body of Christ. Paul warns them, 'That is why many among you are weak and sick and some of you have fallen asleep' (1 Corinthians 11:30, NIV). Corporate anxiety is a seriously damaging emotion which should be ministered to as much as any gross sin. Indeed, left to ferment, it inevitably leads to sins of the Spirit which are far worse.

• **Approval-seeking.** Many times, individuals within an anxiety-ridden congregation will indulge in excessive approval-seeking. Often this will be because an anxious atmosphere does not encourage them to feel loved and valued for themselves. Consequently, the less secure members will attempt to achieve a sense of security by increasing their 'spiritual' performance.

In such circumstances the desire to serve God is subtly transformed into a competition to gain acceptance. Like a child straining to impress a disapproving mother, so people in an anxious environment tend to seek approval from 'the people who matter'. When the group as a whole is anxious for whatever reason, the atmosphere will be brittle and unloving. Anxiety does not promote openness. The less open the members of the body are with each other, the less wanted individuals will feel. One of the few ways left in which to feel wanted is to force recognition by increased effort.

Excessive approval-seeking is an emotional trap. The more we strive for approval, the more anxious we become when approval is not forthcoming. Even when we receive approval there is a strong tendency to analyze it to check whether it is sufficient, whether it is genuine or forced. And so the spiral grows, leading to more and more anxiety. Genuine approval comes from a caring commitment built on an unqualified acceptance of others because of their standing in Christ. The anxious church will know nothing of this. Usually this is because the leaders themselves believe that their standing depends upon performance rather than acceptance. An amazing number of leaders are not secure in Christ. They are performance-orientated because emotionally they do not feel that they are 'accepted in the beloved' to use Paul's phrase.

A BIBLICAL EXAMPLE — THE CORINTHIAN CHURCH

The church at Corinth, in the New Testament, displayed many of the symptoms of an anxious congregation. It is a marvel of God's grace that there was a church at all in Corinth. Both a seaport and a military garrison town, the city was a byword in the ancient world for its immorality. To be called 'a Corinthian' was not a compliment, but suggested that a person was loose-living. Moral laxity, there, was further encouraged by the presence of a massive temple devoted to the goddess Diana. The worship of this temple required the service of hundreds of cultic prostitutes. Small wonder that the infant church established there by the Apostle Paul had to cope with sexual problems.

The fact that Paul was able to address a letter 'to the

Church of God which is at Corinth, to those who are sanctified in Christ Jesus, called to be Saints' (1 Corinthians 1:2, RKJV) is in itself evidence of what God can do. Nor was this any mean church. Paul wrote to them, 'you were enriched in everything by Him in all utterance and in all knowledge, even as the testimony of Christ was confirmed in you, so that you came short in no gift, eagerly awaiting the revelation of our Lord Jesus Christ' (1 Corinthians 1:5 – 7, RKJV). The Corinthian church had a testimony, they knew God's grace, they had eloquent preachers and teachers. Spiritually gifted, they enthusiastically looked for the return of Christ; nevertheless, the church exhibited many of the symptoms of anxiety.

Spirituality and security are not to be attained by correct opinions but by keeping short accounts with God.

• **Correct opinions.** There was an irritability about the Corinthian congregation. As a church, they were split into factions loyal to different teachers and apostles who had made an input into the foundation of the church. That these leaders had no desire to head up splinter groups did not prevent people forming factions. Each group appears to have vied for the superiority of 'their' man. There is an implication that differences of emphasis on the part of successive leaders led the congregation to divide their message. To this Paul replied with the plea 'that you all speak the same thing, and that there be no divisions among you, but that you be perfectly joined together in the same mind and in the same judgement' (1 Corinthians 1:10, RKJV). As Paul pointed out, all truth is common property (3:21 – 23).

The trouble is that the Corinthian Christians were trying to judge the message by the standards of human, worldly wisdom (3:18 – 19), forgetting that there are no competing versions of truth. Truth is finally embodied in Jesus Christ and he is the only foundation for fellowship. Other men build on that foundation. Their wisdom is of a different order which cannot be received naturally. The gifts of the Spirit of God, which these men impart, are spiritually discerned. No amount of wrangling or criticism can establish or dethrone the truth for 'he who is spiritual judges all things, yet he himself is rightly judged by no one' (2:15).

The lesson is clear, people who are anxious to be correct are jockeying for position in the church. They seek to advance their cause by attaching it to the names of leaders. The real problem, however, is that their own carnal or worldly nature has the upper hand. They seek to allay anxiety by correctness of doctrine rather than by commitment to Christ.

Spirituality and security are not to be attained by correct opinions but by keeping short accounts with God. Anxiety for our own interpretation of God's word is born of insecurity based on human wisdom. Doctrinal accuracy can be a cover for sin.

• **Immorality and indecisiveness.** Surrounded as they were by sexual licence and permissiveness, the Corinthian church needed to stand firm on such issues. However, there was a blatant case of immorality between two of their own members. A man was living with his father's wife (probably his step-mother rather than his natural mother). The members of the church said nothing about it. Perhaps they were too embarrassed to take action or maybe they knew what was in their own hearts and feared to judge. Whatever the reason, they responded by inaction — this was one thing in the Corinthian church which nobody talked about!

This situation is paralleled by a church known to us where the organist had an affair with a married woman. In spite of the fact that the church was divided over issues of worship, nothing was said about this moral situation; the church officers took no action. Possibly they were afraid to speak because the organist was the treasurer's son. The father was innocent of what was going on and no one wished to upset him. The congregation seemed unable or unwilling to act. In the same church, one of the deacons attempted a vote of censure on enthusiastic members of the congregation who greeted each other with a hug rather than the more formal handshake!

Whenever a church is divided it becomes reluctant to make strong decisions. The anxiety which is generated in such a fragmented situation causes people to hesitate to act even in cases of open immorality. Indeed, it has been our experience that division in a local congregation is often the result of marital problems among the members.

Whatever the reasons, the church at Corinth was both divided over leadership and insensitive about immorality. The two sources of anxiety caused it to be an indecisive congregation.

• **Quarrelsome Christians.** The Corinthian church may have been unwilling to act over sexual immorality, but individuals within it fell out over secular matters. Moreover, they did it to the point of going to law against each other (see chapter 6). Doctrinal purity was obviously more important than ethical issues. Doctrine which does not lead to purity of conduct is meaningless.

The Corinthian Christians were a quarrelsome bunch. They fell out over teaching and leadership so it isn't surprising to find that they fell out over property. In verse 7 of chapter 6 Paul asks why they do not prefer being defrauded to going to law against a brother. The word 'lawsuit' implies litigation over property or money. Whether their quarrels were over church matters or personal rights, the root cause was the same: each of them was more concerned for himself than for the body of Christ. Personal advancement was more important than spiritual reality.

Paul needed to teach anxious people how to love without standing on their personal rights.

The same attitude is evident in the way in which the Corinthians treated the Lord's Supper and spiritual gifts. Whether it was food brought to the Love Feast or gifts given by the Holy Spirit, their attitude was essentially selfish. The Corinthians were sidetracked by an anxious competitive spirit. The whole of Paul's teaching in relation to the Communion and to spiritual gifts is directed to demonstrating that believers form a body. As members of the same body they were called to serve. Anxious people rarely make good servants, nor do they know how to love, or to be loved. As John comments elsewhere: 'perfect love casts out fear, because fear involves torment' (1 John 4:18). In fact, as John says, love knows no fear. Anxiety is a condition of fear, it is therefore difficult for anxious people to love. This is why Paul penned his incomparable passage on love in 1 Corinthians chapter 13. He needed to teach anxious people how to love without standing on their personal rights. We might say in paraphrase:

> Anxiety is impatient and unkind; anxiety envies the success of others, loves to parade itself because of its insecurity, in a curious way inflates the sufferer's own importance; behaves rudely, seeks its own advantage, is

easily provoked and readily believes the worst of others,
it rejoices in iniquity, is sceptical about the truth;
anxiety cracks under burdens, doubts at every turn,
loses its grasp on hope, whether for itself or others, is
unable to endure pressures. Anxiety always fails
therefore love is the only antidote.

It is worth noting that for a church as rich in spiritual gifts
as the church at Corinth, a turnabout is possible. The atmosphere evident at Corinth by the time Paul wrote his fourth
letter to them (our 2 Corinthians) was very different. The
reason is because they were willing to respond to the Lord.
Recognizing Paul's apostolic authority, they repented and
responded to God's word to them. In the end they allowed
the Holy Spirit to have his way.

3

DEVELOPMENT

How Anxiety Grows

5

Destructive Anxiety

I still remember starting my first full-time job. As a teenager, fresh out of school, I made my way with a crowd of other workers through the factory gate. Uncertain of myself, I seemed to be the only one unsure of what to do. Through the alley-way at the top of the yard was the entrance to the laboratories where I was to begin work as a trainee laboratory technician. A group of men in white overalls streamed by and a knot of laughing factory girls unceremoniously jostled past the bewildered youth, trying to find his bearings.

What will it be like, working in an adult world? I thought. How will I get on with the other workers? My throat went dry, my stomach muscles contracted, Can I retain all the new information? Will I be able to cope? My science grades in the final school examinations were not brilliant. Had I made a mistake in choosing this job?

Even now, I can recall how anxious and uncertain I was on that first day at work. I mentally ran over all the possibilities (and impossibilities!) which the day might bring.

Although I felt really grown up, perhaps for the first time in my life, I also dreaded what might follow.

Fortunately, my fears were short-lived. A senior technician met me at the door and introduced me to Ivan, one of his juniors. Ivan had worked for the Chemical Corporation for just two years. In fact he had passed through the same school ahead of me so I knew him vaguely. He quickly showed me the clocking in procedure and took me round the plant, introducing me to my new colleagues. I soon began to settle down to a new routine. It wasn't so bad after all.

Scenes of normal anxiety such as this one are everyday occurrences, all over the world. The level of anxiety experienced is relatively mild. It merely keys us up for action. Without it we would not be alert and capable. Many preachers know what it is to make frequent trips to the bathroom before a speaking engagement! Mild anxiety states such as these enable us to anticipate what we are about to face and cause us to be mentally limbered up to meet it effectively.

Normal anxiety makes us aware of changes, needs and problems. Such anxiety is usually discharged when it is channelled into appropriate action. Undischarged anxiety is unhealthy; it becomes a gnawing, free-floating fear which debilitates, preventing the sufferer from meeting the realities of life head on.

TRIGGERS OF DESTRUCTIVE ANXIETY

Destructive anxiety of this second type — anxiety which has not been resolved in action — usually lurks beneath the surface until it eventually breaks out into an anxiety-state. An anxiety-state is a condition in which anxiety results in serious physical or psychological symptoms. These symptoms may erupt suddenly and without warning. Often there will be no apparent or logical explanation for them.

In acute cases the sufferer may vomit, become rigid or pass into unconsciousness. More commonly he alone will be aware of the symptoms. For instance, the person in an anxiety-state may feel unable to move his limbs in the face of danger. Like a wild animal caught in the headlights, he is transfixed even when there are no visible outward symptoms of his fear.

There are five common triggers of anxiety-states. We will now look at these, giving biblical and contemporary examples to illustrate them.

1. Threats to personal goals

An anxiety-state can be brought about when the sufferer experiences a threat to his personal goals. A sudden change of status or direction in life can constitute such a threat. Most of us have a conscious or unconscious set of values for our lives. These may consist of aspirations or ambitions. Often they will relate to our career but, for some people, other goals may be more important than our job prospects.

In the Old Testament book of Esther, Haman had two personal goals which were complementary. One was to advance his own prestige in the Persian Empire of King Ahasuerus (in some Bible translations he is called Xerxes). The other was to exterminate the Jews. By presenting the Jews as an unidentified public enemy, Haman hoped to offer himself as the saviour of the Persian Empire. He thus persuaded the King to pass an edict to annihilate the Jews, little knowing that Queen Esther was herself Jewish.

When Queen Esther discovered the plot she invited Haman and her husband to a private meal. Haman began to believe that the fulfilment of his ambitions were in sight:

> Haman went out that day joyful and glad of heart...[he] went home and fetched his friends and his wife Zeresh. And Haman recounted to them the splendour of his riches, the number of his sons, all the promotions with which the King had honoured him, and how he had advanced him above the princes and servants of the King. And Haman added, 'Even Queen Esther let no one come with the king to the banquet she prepared, but myself. And tomorrow also I am invited by her, together with the King. Yet all this does me no good, so long as I see Mordecai the Jew, sitting at the King's gate.' Then his wife Zeresh and all his friends said to him, 'Let a gallows fifty cubits high be made, and in the morning tell the King to have Mordecai hanged upon it; then go merrily with the King to dinner.' This counsel pleased Haman and he had the gallows made.

Clearly Haman saw the banquet as the pinnacle of all his ambitions. As a result of it he would be further honoured and his arch-enemy Mordecai, Esther's guardian, would be destroyed. However, at the banquet, Esther revealed the plot to her husband, the King, who was furious. Haman grovelled before the Queen for his life to be spared. In his anxiety to curry favour, Haman fell across Esther's couch. Ahasuerus thought that Haman was assaulting his Queen. In his fury, he pointed to the gallows,

> And the King said, 'Hang him on that.' So they hanged Haman on the gallows which he had prepared for Mordecai. *(from* Esther, *chapters 6 and 7,* TEV)

Everything that Haman desired seemed to be within his reach but, in one short step, all his personal goals were threatened. His status was in danger of being reduced to nothing. From a haughty, apparently successful adviser who believed he could control events, Haman quickly became an abject coward wailing for his life! Eventually, he was hanged on the gallows of his own ambitions.

This may be an extreme case, but whenever strongly-held personal goals are jeopardized, men are reduced to moral impotence and, frequently, illness. It is all a question of where we place our trust.

KEN'S STORY

And now, a contemporary case study, which illustrates the same theme of the threat to personal goals. Ken was a successful planning engineer working with a large firm. Approaching the age of fifty it seemed that the top positions in his field were opening up to him. He threw himself into his work and found great satisfaction in it. He prided himself in the quality of his work and in the time which he gave to his employers.

Since he was immersed in his job, Ken failed to notice that external economic conditions were changing. Soon the firm was forced to restructure and Ken's career mobility was radically altered. Instead of an attractive promotion ladder he was confronted with a career plateau and maybe even the possibility of redundancy. The prospect depressed Ken. He began to lose interest in his work. Because he could not face the lack of advancement, he became nervous and irritable at home. Before long he began to take tranquillizers and was unable to cope with responsibility in his marriage. Life became unbearable and when redundancy terms were offered by his company, he found it difficult to make a decision.

Ken became a sick man because his status was threatened. Most of his self-esteem was locked up in his work and the possibility of 'getting on' in his career. Although he was a Christian, God was not the directing force in his life.

Ambition had become a substitute for relationships, particularly for his relationship with God and his own wife. Eventually, Ken was taken to a church where he was not known and a 'word of wisdom' was brought direct to him during a worship service. Not until then did he realize that his illness was triggered by the betrayal of false values. He has since attempted to work out a new way of life, controlled by Christ, which would lead him to wholeness.

2. *Dangerous desires*

A second trigger point which can provoke an anxiety-state is when dangerous desires threaten to break through into a person's consciousness. Frequently we harbour desires which we know to be wrong. Rather than dealing with them, we tend to repress them, submerging our desires beneath other thoughts. The more our desires trouble us, the more we push them down and as these desires are pressed out of sight they become compacted beneath the surface of the mind and, like a seething volcano, small eruptions take place. Every passionate thought gives rise to greater anxiety about the newly-suppressed emotions. This anxiety, in turn, adds to the pressure which threatens a final, devastating, blow out.

There are many ways in which we can deal with the threatened outbreak of dangerous desires. When the pressure becomes intolerable, the body or mind will react. Often the reaction will be in a form which immobilizes the will, preventing the patient from expressing his desires. God turned Lot's wife into a pillar of salt because she looked back with longing desire towards Sodom. More frequently the punishment is self-inflicted. The patient becomes as arid and immobile as Lot's wife.

For instance, Patsy came for counselling because she would periodically fall into a cataleptic trance. Sometimes in dangerous circumstances her body would become rigid and, unless she was injected with muscle relaxants, she would remain paralyzed for several hours.

Fortunately Patsy's minister was a trained counsellor and a medical practitioner. He was able to gently probe her spiritual problem. Even so, her case baffled him until he asked God for a word of knowledge which would unlock her needs. Patsy was a skilled shorthand typist so one day, on the pretext of lack of office help, the Pastor dictated Patsy's own case notes to her. In the middle of a description of her condition he interjected the word of knowledge which had to do with sexual fantasies. Immediately, Patsy stiffened up, her body became rigid and, in the presence of her parents, she slid under the table! After a muscle relaxant was administered, Patsy confessed her sin and received forgiveness from God. Subsequently, she prayed for the infilling of the Holy Spirit and was shown how to deal with wayward thoughts and emotions. Over twenty years later she has not experienced another attack. The trance was her body's way of coping with a problem which her mind could no longer handle. Patsy has found out how to face up to dangerous desires and overcome them in the name of Christ. She is learning to take every thought captive to make it obedient to Christ (2 Corinthians 10:5).

In 2 Samuel, chapter 13, an Old Testament example of the breakthrough of dangerous desires is found in the conduct of Amnon with his half-sister, Tamar. Amnon, one of King David's sons, physically desired his half-sister Tamar to the point that he became downcast and sick. One of his friends noticed this and, when he discovered the cause, concocted a plan to enable Amnon to seduce Tamar. Amnon ended up, after the seduction, hating Tamar and blaming her for his conduct. His anxiety over his actions led Amnon to project the guilt onto the innocent party in this affair.

A more faithful counsellor than Amnon's toadying friend would have shown that this former sickness and despair were probably due to guilt-ridden anxiety. This would have been better dealt with by confession and the submission of these dangerous desires to God's control. Better to be sick than sinful, but there was no need for either. The real mistake came from harbouring such dangerous desires in the first place. (They inevitably lead to further sin or sickness; sometimes to both.)

Amnon's father, David, had earlier graphically described the results of anxiety due to hiding the effects of such dangerous desires. After his own affair with Bathsheba was discovered, David reported the effects of suppressing sin in the words of Psalm 32:3 – 4:

> When I kept silent,
> my bones wasted away
> through my groaning all the day long.
> For day and night
> your hand was heavy upon me;
> my strength was sapped
> as in the heat of summer.

Later, in consequence of a courageous confrontation by Nathan the prophet, David turned to God. One senses David's relief when he realizes he was caught out. He records:

> Then I acknowledged my sin to you,
> and did not cover up my iniquity,
> I said, 'I will confess my transgressions to the Lord' —
> and you forgave the guilt of my sin.
>
> *(Psalm 32:5,* NIV*)*

The three guilt-words which David used to describe his actions are instructive:

- 'my sin' — failure

- 'my iniquity' — an attitude
- 'my transgression' — an act

Just so, anxiety over dangerous desires is a sin. The Hebrew word represented by 'sin' means 'to miss a target'. Dangerous desires arise from a failure to control our thoughts. Such anxiety, when prolonged, becomes iniquity. The word we have as 'iniquity' basically means 'lawlessness', so our dangerous desires develop into an unprincipled attitude of which we are afraid. This attitude heightens the anxiety brought on by the initial failure to control our thoughts. Third, the anxiety caused by this attitude, if unchecked, will inevitably lead to transgression. The original word means 'to break out of bounds'. It indicates an act which is the result of an attitude boiling over into uncontrolled action and emotion. If an emotional outbreak does not occur, the repressed attitudes will, instead, surface as an illness. In some cases, as King David testified, they lead both to evil acts and to illness brought about by a further bout of guilty anxiety.

Anxiety caused by attempts to cover up the consequences of our dangerous desires is sin, an undirected driving release of our desires. Conversely, sanctification comes about from a controlled release of those desires to God so that our sins are covered.

3. Anxiety-arousing decisions

One of the most common triggers of anxiety is the need to make important decisions. Some people thrive on decision-making. They have an inbuilt sense that making decisions is necessary to mental, moral and spiritual growth. Other people fear making up their mind because they cannot cope with the possibility of being wrong. They are the victims of an inner drive towards perfection which, perversely, paralyzes their ability to succeed. Such a person feels that if he makes the wrong decision he will violate his compulsion towards perfection. If his perfectionism is thwarted in this way, he will not be able to accept himself. So it becomes painful to decide.

In some forms, the drive to perfection is tied up with a desire for approval from others, 'What will they think of me if I do the wrong thing?' In some cultures this is bound up with the idea of 'loss of face'. This fear of failure means that it is better to hide behind protocol, convention or etiquette than to be a real person. It is better to obtain the approval of others at the price of becoming a cardboard cut-out than it is to risk expressing oneself at the cost of making occasional wrong decisions.

The trouble is that the approval one earns in this way is always teetering on the brink of disapproval. 'Suppose I read the signs wrongly and break the conventions? Will I still be accepted then?' An unwillingness to take risks results in treading a path through life which is a moral minefield. The consequence is an inability to make any decision unless forced to it. Such people are blown to and fro by every wind of social doctrine.

Some life-decisions are momentous and require careful thought but there are few decisions, honestly made, from which we cannot recover if they go wrong. Indeed such recoveries constitute some of life's most important character-building experiences.

Most decisions are of a less momentous sort and can be taken with less heart-searching thought. If our lives are laid on the right guiding principles, many of these decisions will hardly require any thought. The thinking will already have been done. In this way we can concentrate on the more important issues when they arise. Those who dither about decisions are often swayed by feelings of failure and non-acceptance, feelings which give rise to increasing anxiety.

It is a poor thing to be swayed by popularity rather than principle.

Pontius Pilate represents this kind of person. When confronted by the demand to find Jesus guilty, he could not do so on the evidence. However, he feared for his career and for how things would look if he made a decision which could lead to riot or rebellion. Wavering between principle and expediency, he washed his hands as a symbol that the decision wasn't really his. It was like backing both horses in a two-horse race! He couldn't both refuse to decide and refuse to accept responsibility. But this is what people often do, failing to realize that not to decide is itself a decision. Pilate must have been a very anxious man. He faced pressures from his wife, pressures from Rome and pressures from his conscience. In the end he took the safe course. Tradition would have us believe it ended in personal disaster, for he is alleged to have committed suicide.

4. Reactivation of prior traumas

A fourth trigger of anxiety is when old shocks or wounds have been healed over lightly and they are suddenly re-activated. Often this will occur when the conditions in which the wound was first sustained are paralleled or repeated.

For instance, a trapeze artiste dropped by her partner during practice will experience extreme anxiety when the same routine is performed before a crowd. This will happen even when she is working with a new partner. If the routine is to be performed with the same person who failed the catch, anxiety will be heightened even more.

In just the same way, a middle-aged wife whose husband has been caught in an illicit affair with his young secretary, will become very anxious when he takes on new office staff. Even a truthful telephone call to say that her husband has been detained late at the office will give rise to pain and anguish.

Similarly, a congregation whose brilliant young pastor has suffered a moral lapse will tend to be anxious at the thought of appointing another young man. Any number of examples will be brought to mind where an 'action replay' of an event will reactivate the anxiety aroused at the time of the original action.

A young man in one church was unable to accept authority. His attitude to other people in leadership was stubborn and uncooperative. The only leadership to which he was able to relate was of the permissive variety. As soon as he came alongside any leader who was clearly self-disciplined and likely to make demands upon him, he rebelled. Sometimes he would even cause a scene.

On investigation it turned out that as a child he had been sent to a boarding school by his parents. On the day that he was first left at school he kicked and screamed because he wanted to go home with his father. The Principal held the boy down while his father left the room. The boy grew up resenting authority and rejecting the self-discipline required for learning because he associated it with authority. He gradually interpreted discipline as a denial of enjoyment and authority as personal rejection. Secure personalities made him feel unhappy and he veered away from strong leaders so that they would not have the chance to reject him.

The circumstances of this man's church life were not the same as his experience of school but they were sufficiently similar to provoke extreme anxiety. The pity is that he himself had good leadership potential.

In the same way, divorced people tend to distance themselves from church involvement of anything but a formal kind. In one setting they have been let down in a close relationship. It hurts too much to allow themselves to be put into another set of circumstances which could also end in disaster. They steer clear of warm fellowship because they are anxious about the possibility of emotional rejection. And churches who receive them go through the same kind of anxiety.

The way to deliverance from anxiety in such circumstances is not to avoid the situation. A creative re-enactment of the anxiety situation which gave rise to the original trauma can help immensely. To take an example from the New Testament, it was in just such a way that Jesus walked by the misty lake early in the morning (John 21). As he walked, he paused and said, 'Peter, do you love me?' Peter's anxiety was aroused as he remembered his earlier protestations of loyalty and his consequent failure. Peter must have been hurt. Nevertheless, Jesus persisted with the question three times, reminding Peter of his three verbal denials of his master. Each time, Peter was allowed to re-affirm his love. It was then that he was able to face his failure and find forgiveness, for in each affirmation he received a fresh token of the Lord's trust — 'Feed my lambs...take care of my sheep...feed my sheep.' Jesus ended with the absolution of a re-commissioning which would re-activate, not the wounds in Peter's heart, but the joy with which he first encountered the Lord. For Jesus concluded the interview by saying, 'Follow me!'

On the way, he indicated that Peter would encounter further wounds but that they would not matter. Indeed, by them he would glorify God.

5. *Guilt and fear of punishment*

The final trigger of an anxiety-state is a strong sense of guilt and the fear of punishment that goes with it.

In a permissive society, has our sense of guilt been totally lost? It is true that there are no longer any commonly agreed standards of conduct, but everyone has some inbuilt set of rules or a code of behaviour. These may have been acquired during child-rearing or they may, less commonly, have been thought through and adopted deliberately. Either way, few of us live up to the ethics we have acquired. This failure leaves many people with an underlying sense of guilt. This can be compounded when our standards are implied rather than consciously worked out. This makes the sense of guilt difficult to pin down.

In fact, a prominent group of New York-based psychiatrists say guilt is the cause of a high proportion of their cases. They claim that many breakdowns, and probably a large number of psychosomatic illnesses, are due to feelings of unassuaged guilt.

If we have no way of dealing with guilt we suppress it until it can no longer be contained.

This should not surprise us. For the most part our sense of right and wrong is acquired during childhood. Child-rearing practices are, rightly, reinforced by some system of reward or punishment. Mild punishment, whether verbal or otherwise, serves to teach values, but when that punishment is either over-strict or erratic, it can cause problems. On the one hand, excessively strict sanctions can give rise to a punctilious correctness and a rigid personality, and a victim of this is likely to carry around a sense of guilty failure. On the other hand, erratically applied sanctions can cause moral uncertainty accompanied by a fear of punishment. Often the punishment will be self-inflicted in the form of emotional or physical illness.

If we have no way of dealing with guilt we suppress it until it can no longer be contained. Even when it is submerged, a strong sense of guilt can give rise to feelings of general uneasiness and anxiety. Unless our guilt is dealt with and we are freed from it, we will attempt to make reparation for ourselves, involving self-blame and some form of self-punishment. In the most extreme cases the sufferer will break out into an anxiety-state which can take many forms. Guilt-ridden people may become neurotic or psychotic. Unless the guilt is dealt with there is likely to be some psychic or physical damage.

CHRYSTAL'S STORY

Chrystal loved her father, although she did not show it clearly. During her adolescence she kicked over the traces, rebelling against her parents, causing them a great deal of heartache. (Chrystal's father was not a Christian, although her mother was.) Chrystal had herself made a commitment to Christ before she began to rebel. During the period of rebellion, Chrystal's father became ill with a duodenal ulcer. He did not adhere strictly to the prescribed treatment and one day the ulcer perforated and he died.

Chrystal's mother felt guilty that she hadn't done more to lead her husband to Christ. She began to niggle at her daughter, telling her that ulcers are caused by worry. She strongly implied that Chrystal's behaviour led directly to her father's death. Chrystal ended up blaming herself, feeling that she had never returned to her father's love and had thereby killed him. She was unable to forgive herself and she sought for love and acceptance elsewhere. Her conduct with a series of boy-friends left her feeling more and more guilty. Eventually she suffered a complete breakdown. She was unable to believe God could forgive her since her mother hadn't and, finally, she attempted suicide.

Since receiving professional psychiatric treatment Chrystal

has learned to cope better with life. However, it is only as she has been confronted with the Word of God and its demands to accept real, not imagined, responsibility that she has been able to accept the love of God. She is beginning to find out how to deal with self-accusation and discriminate between it and real guilt. Gradually she has found the answer to both through a deepening faith in Christ.

The Bible indicates the difference between remorse and repentance. The Apostle Paul points out that 'Godly sorrow brings repentance that leads to salvation and leaves no regret, but worldly sorrow brings death' (2 Corinthians 7:10, NIV). Sorrow may stem from anxiety but there is a world of difference between remorse and repentance. Remorse led Judas Iscariot to commit suicide whereas repentance turned Saul of Tarsus into Paul the Apostle, perhaps the greatest missionary that ever lived.

WHERE DO WE STAND?

Anxiety is a killer, it can bring us to an untimely grave through sickness, suicide or breakdown. In its more extreme forms it will render us incapable of effective spiritual effort. Prominent Christians and even whole congregations have been paralyzed by fear and anxiety which has prevented them from reaching their potential.

Dr Paul Yongi-Cho is the Korean Pastor of the world's largest congregation in Seoul, currently numbering in excess of 500,000 members. In his book *The Fourth Dimension* Yongi-Cho recalls how at one point in his ministry he over-extended himself financially. Left with a half-finished building, soaring debts and a congregation which was beginning to desert him, he contemplated suicide. Anxious about what people thought of his failure, he attempted to throw himself out of the window of his apartment. However, God spoke to him clearly, showing that this course of action would be an evasion of responsibility. Yongi-Cho faced up to his failure and the anxieties which it brought. He accepted the call of God upon his life and the Lord's ability to enable him to overcome. By determined effort and commitment to the purposes of God for his life, he was able to turn anxiety-ridden failure into a determination to be steadfast.

We too can either stand upon our own view of ourselves, conditioned by past experiences, or we can stand upon what God the Father thinks of us. Remember, his estimation of us is that it was worth sending his Son to die for us. Where are we going to stand?

6

Insecurity and Anxiety

C huck did not come from a deprived background in the material sense. Nevertheless, his mother was severe with him, frequently beating him when he was naughty as a child. It seemed to Chuck that his mother preferred his younger sister and often he was blamed, and punished, for things which his sister had done.

In adult life Chuck was unsure of himself although he was good at his job. When his boss offered him promotion to become line-manager he turned it down in favour of remaining on the shop-floor. Starved of affection, he married early but was never able to give affection to his wife or to believe that she loved him. He handed over family finances and management to her because he was afraid of the responsibility. At the same time he resented his wife's competence.

Chuck's sense of inadequacy was deepened because his sister was academically successful and continued to be held up by their mother as a model to follow. When his mother divorced, Chuck left his wife and went back home to his mother to live. It was as though he was striving to win back the affection and security he had craved from her as a child. Chuck had not yet grown up emotionally.

Feelings of insecurity arouse great anxiety and are not infrequently the cause of apparently inexplicable behaviour. In fact, underlying the five triggers of anxiety which we discussed in the last chapter, is often a sense of insecurity.

ABILITY TO COPE

There are many reasons why people may become insecure. Sometimes an increase in responsibility or the apparent withdrawal of approval will make a person feel insecure. As I write this I have just returned from a Baptist Ministers' fraternal at which two out of the twelve men present revealed that they were being forced to resign because their ministry was not appreciated. A third was being cross-examined by his board of deacons. Each of these men exhibited clear symptoms of distress brought on by a sense of rejection and the insecurity which this carries. Although their basic security was in Christ they, nevertheless, felt insecure and anxious in their ministry.

Some people feel insecure when they are promoted at work. They worry about their ability to cope and whether they will be accepted by those over whom they have been promoted. These feelings will be heightened if failed candidates for the post are now asked to work under them. Will their support be withdrawn in these circumstances?

Frequently these fears prove to be unfounded but this does not necessarily result in a reduction of anxiety. One example of this spiral of insecure anxiety can be found by following events in the life of King Saul in the Old Testament.

SPIRITUAL AWARENESS

The first thing that must be said about Saul is that his spiritual awareness was never finely developed. There were moments when he was overtaken by the Spirit of God and when, in spite of himself, he gave rein to the more spiritual side of his nature. But, right from the beginning when we come upon him looking for his father's missing donkeys, he seemed to have little awareness of spiritual realities (see 1 Samuel, chapter 9). When they had wandered far from home on their fruitless quest it was the servant who suggested they turn aside to consult the man of God. When they met Samuel, Saul did not know who he was. There cannot have been many men in Israel at the time who were not aware of Samuel and his ministry, since he was the only man through whom words from the Lord were coming!

At later points in his life, when he had become King, Saul exhibited the same spiritual carelessness. When he was told to wait for Samuel at Gilgal before Israel's conflict with the Philistines he could not hold on. Instead he thrust himself into the prophet's role and offered sacrifice himself. This was purely for political reasons, to prevent his men from deserting. Again, when told to deal with the Amalekites Saul obeyed only partially. He thought he knew better than God. Once more, his motive was to keep in with his troops. In this we can see signs of anxiety over his position as king.

The same symptoms appear in his reaction to Goliath's threats and in his relationship with David. Saul's anxiety prevailed throughout his life because he was not secure in God. Eventually, this led to the withdrawal of the Spirit of God from him.

EQUIPMENT FOR THE JOB

When the young Saul and his servant consulted the prophet Samuel at Zuph, the prophet recognized the fulfilment of a word from God.

> Now the day before Saul came, the Lord had revealed this to Samuel: 'About this time tomorrow I will send you a man from the land of Benjamin. Anoint him leader over my people Israel; he will deliver my people from the hand of the Philistines. I have looked upon my people, for their cry has reached me.' When Samuel caught sight of Saul, the Lord said to him, 'This is the man I spoke to you about; he will govern my people.'
>
> *1 Samuel 9:15 – 17,* NIV

Subsequently, Samuel anointed Saul and pointed to a series of signs which would be fulfilled before his Kingship was realized. One of these signs was that Saul would meet a band of prophets and then, 'The Spirit of the Lord will come upon you in power, and you will prophesy with them: and you will be changed into a different person.' We read that, 'As Saul turned to leave Samuel, God changed Saul's heart, and all these signs were fulfilled that day' (1 Samuel 10:6 – 9). What took place was so uncharacteristic of Saul that, 'When all those who had formerly known him saw him prophesying with the prophets, they asked each other, "What is this that has happened to the Son of Kish? Is Saul also among the prophets?"' (1 Samuel 10:11). In fact, we are told that the question, 'Is Saul also among the prophets?' became a kind of sceptical catch-phrase!

Saul had the equipment for the job to which he was appointed. When he is introduced into the story it says, 'Saul [was] an impressive young man without equal among the Israelites — a head taller than any of the others' (1 Samuel 9:2). There we have it: Saul was physically and intellectually impressive but spiritually deficient, until God anointed him through the prophet, changed his heart, and empowered him by the Holy Spirit. Surely there was nothing to prevent him living a life of success?

It was Saul's responsibility to choose whether to live in the anointing and spiritual empowering from God or to rely on his natural abilities. Unfortunately, he mostly fell back on his own resources and this is what caused insecurity to predominate and anxiety to mount. Saul's life is a picture of the battle between the spirit and the flesh — a battle known to all of us.

UNCERTAINTY AND IMPATIENCE

The next stage in the appointment of Saul as king over Israel was to secure the support of the people. The prophet Samuel called the nation together and cast lots to arrive at the name of the man of God's choice. When the choice narrowed down to Saul's tribe, clan and family and finally to Saul himself, he was nowhere to be found. It took a word from the Lord to reveal that Saul was hiding among the baggage in the camp!

Apparently, Saul was not ready to face the responsibility. In spite of all that had gone before, the preparation that God had put in, and the encouragement that Saul had received through the fulfilment of prophecy, he still hid.

There is more than a hint in the narrative that when Saul was found, attention was drawn to his physique. Perhaps this reinforced his tendency to rely on his own natural ability. He would have done better to have stayed with the distrust of his own abilities which led him to hide in the first place, even though this was born of insecurity. Or perhaps Saul distrusted the supernatural equipment he had received from God.

At his selection Saul won the hearts of some valiant men,

touched by God, even though others despised him. When the first test of his kingship came, Saul rose to the occasion with a rallying call to Israel who willingly followed. Natural ability and spiritual response came together; as Saul experienced the Spirit of God coming upon him in power he burned with anger at the Ammonite treatment of the city of Jabesh. His anger was controlled, however, and with brilliant military strategy he routed the Ammonites and rescued Jabesh. Before his ensuing coronation the victors urged Saul to put the gainsayers in his Kingdom to death but Saul responded nobly, 'No one shall be put to death today,' he said, 'for this day the Lord has rescued Israel.'

This was Saul at his finest. He did not rely upon natural ability to establish himself as king or to win the battle. At the end of the day he gave honour to God. If Saul had continued as he began, the story of his reign would have been entirely different.

It was as though Saul could rely upon God when the issues were clear-cut. But when the situation was more uncertain he gave way to insecurity and felt forced to act out of anxiety.

Saul's insecurity arose because he had not consulted God in the first place.

For instance, when his son Jonathan attacked a Philistine outpost, Saul felt compelled to call Israel to arms. He had not consulted God about this move. When the Philistines mustered they were numerically superior to the Israelites and they were far better equipped. It was a bit like the Hungarian uprising of 1956 where the populace fought Russian tanks with rifle fire, rocks and hand-grenades. 'When the men of Israel saw that their situation was critical and that their army was hard pressed, they hid in caves and thickets, among the rocks and in pits and cisterns. Some Hebrews even crossed the Jordan to the land of Gad and Gilead' (1 Samuel 13:6 – 7).

Saul, at least, remained at Gilgal with some of his men, where Samuel had arranged a rendezvous with him. However, 'the troops with him were quaking with fear.' When Samuel overshot the appointed time by seven days, Saul went ahead and offered the sacrifices himself whereupon Samuel turned up.

When Samuel questioned him as to his action Saul defended himself. 'When I saw the men were scattering, and that you did not come at the set time, and that the Philistines were assembling at Michmash, I thought, "Now the Philistines will come down against me at Gilgal, and I have not sought the Lord's favour." So I felt compelled to offer the burnt offering' (1 Samuel 13:11 – 12).

Saul's insecurity arose because he had not consulted God in the first place. He sought God's favour as an afterthought, when things appeared to be going wrong. The whole enterprise was forged in the realm of good ideas and personal feelings. God was being used as a political pawn. No wonder it ended in disaster. How contemporary it all sounds — too often our insecurity arises out of our attempts to serve God in our own way instead of his. To do this is to invite uncertainty which inevitably, as in the case of Saul, leads us to act impatiently. When we merely ask God to bless what we have already decided to do, we should not be too surprised when the answer is delayed.

PARTIAL OBEDIENCE

Saul's encounter with the Amalekites reveals another facet of his character, a development of his fatal flaw. The instructions which he received from the Lord were clear and unequivocal: because of their sins Saul was to destroy the Amalekites totally and everything that belonged to them. But Saul equivocated, 'He took Agag, King of the Amalekites alive, and all his people he totally destroyed with the sword. But Saul and the army spared Agag and the best of the sheep and cattle, the fat calves and lambs — everything that was good. These they were unwilling to destroy completely, but everything that was despised and weak they totally destroyed' (1 Samuel 15:8 – 9).

Saul used his natural reason to sit in judgement upon God. He decided what out of God's instructions made sense and what did not. Furthermore, Saul's former distrust of his own ability had by now disappeared. In fact his confidence in his own abilities had developed to the point of vanity. When Samuel searched him out he was told, 'Saul has gone to Carmel. There he has set up a monument in his own honour and has turned and gone on down to Gilgal' (1 Samuel 15:12).

When Samuel caught up with Saul he accused him of partial obedience and, to Samuel, the man of God, partial obedience was no obedience at all. Saul tried to justify his action, firstly by blaming his troops and secondly by appealing to the religious motivation behind their act. 'I completely destroyed the Amalekites and brought back Agag their King,' he said. 'The soldiers took sheep and cattle from the plunder, the best of what was devoted to God, in order to sacrifice them to the Lord your God at Gilgal' (verses 20 – 21). The phrase 'the Lord *your* God' is revealing; perhaps Saul was criticizing Samuel's view of God or, more likely, he was indicating that he already sensed a distance between God and himself.

Samuel's reply nailed the subterfuge, 'Does the Lord delight in burnt offerings and sacrifices as much as obeying the Lord?' he asked. 'To obey is better than to sacrifice and

to heed is better than the fat of rams. For rebellion is like
the sin of divination, and arrogance like the evil of idolatry'
(verses 22 – 23). This sounds harsh, but in going his own
way Saul had joined the enemy. What the Amalekites were
to be punished for was the ultimate conclusion of the line
which Saul was now following. He thought that he knew
better than God, and in the process he both failed to do
what he had been asked and did what he had not been told
to do — rebellion and arrogance indeed. It may be argued
that Saul had obeyed God to an extent. But as far as God is
concerned, partial obedience is no obedience at all.

Rebellion and arrogance seem light years away from insecurity but in reality they are often quite close. This was certainly so in Saul's case. The problem was, he wanted people
to think well of him. This can be seen in his action in setting up a monument to himself and in his desire to please
his men. In his confession to Samuel Saul admitted, 'I have
sinned, I violated the Lord's command and your instructions.
I was afraid of the people and so I gave in to them. Now I
beg you, forgive my sin and come back with me, so that I
may worship the Lord' (verses 24 – 25).

**Rebellion and arrogance seem light years
away from insecurity but in reality they are
often quite close.**

Saul's repentance was shallow. He assumed that the
prophet was in a position to do what only God could do —
forgive. He was more concerned with appearances than
with reality. Even when Samuel pronounced God's judgement and told him that the Lord had rejected him as king of
Israel, Saul assumed that the opinion of the people was
more important. 'I have sinned,' he confessed, 'But please
honour me before the elders of my people and before Israel;

come back with me so that I may worship the Lord your God' (verse 30).

Apparently Saul was so insecure about his standing with the nation that he could not take in his rejection by God. Samuel graciously did not undermine Saul's position by making this rejection public. To do so would have destroyed the King prematurely. If Saul's uncertainty about his standing had been less pronounced, he would not have acted so impatiently. The real reason for Saul's insecurity with those he tried to lead was that he had no deep sense of security in God, who had provided him with supernatural power if only he chose to use it.

FEAR OF FAILURE

God's rejection went deeper with Saul than it would at first appear. We later read that the Spirit of the Lord departed from him and that an injurious spirit affected him. Saul paid dearly for his anxious rebellion. He lost touch with reality in more senses than one. Despair gave way to depressive moods and it was at this point that David came into contact with the King, brought in to play soothing music to him.

We next see Saul on the battlefield again, this time confronted by Goliath. In chapter 17, the impudent challenge to single combat sent Saul and his entourage into a spin. 'On hearing the Philistine's words, Saul and all the Israelites were dismayed and terrified.' Prior to this Saul had not lacked courage in battle. It seems that when he contemplated the size of the opponent, Saul knew he did not have the physical ability to meet the demands. What he appears to have feared was the thought of failure in full view of both sides. Saul's attitudes were shared by his army. Leaders frequently impart their own confidence or uncertainty to their followers.

When David came on the scene, although he was relatively young, he did not share the view of his countrymen. His perspective was different. The soldiers ran in fear when Goliath issued his challenge. 'Do you see how this man keeps coming out?' they asked, 'He comes out to defy Israel.' But David saw things otherwise. 'Who is this uncircumcised Philistine that he should defy the armies of the living God?' he said.

For David an insult against the nation was an insult against God. So he went to meet the Philistine, rejecting the security of arms and armour. David went out on the attack for God. In the end he did not rely on his natural skill with the sling.

> David said to the Philistine, 'You come against me with sword and spear and javelin, but I come against you in the name of the Lord Almighty, the God of the armies of Israel, whom you have defied. This day the Lord will hand you over to me, and I will strike you down and cut off your head. Today I will give the carcasses of the Philistine army to the birds of the air and the beasts of the earth, and the whole world will know that there is a God in Israel.'
> *1 Samuel 17:45 – 46*

This was big talk but it was possible because David had a big God. Unlike Saul, David did not contemplate failure because his cause was identified with that of his God.

PERSONAL ECLIPSE

Saul was, of course, grateful for the results of David's faith and courage. However, he was not pleased when the victorious army was welcomed home by the women dancing in the streets to the catchy little refrain:

**Saul has slain his thousands,
and David his tens of thousands.**
1 Samuel 18:7

We read, 'Saul was very angry; this refrain galled him. "They have credited David with tens of thousands," he thought, "but me with only thousands. What more can he get but the Kingdom?" And from that time on Saul kept a jealous eye on David' (verses 8 – 9). This means that Saul worked for the praise of women. Their accolades were more important to him than his calling by God.

At this point Saul dared not make his anger known, since David was so popular. Popularity was what he himself had always courted. In it lay his security, and when it was transferred to another Saul could not cope. His anxiety mounted, feeding the jealousy with which he hounded David for the rest of his reign.

The remainder of Saul's story is a sordid account of his attempts to dislodge David from public popularity. Driven by his jealousy he made himself look foolish by his heavy-handed attempts to liquidate the one man everyone else knew was loyal to him. Saul feared an eclipse of his personal position so much that it obsessed him.

Because of this attitude Samuel had withdrawn his support sometime before. When Samuel died, Saul, in a fit of reforming enthusiasm, banished all the mediums and spiritists from the land. Faced with yet one more threat from the Philistines, we find Saul isolated from his closest advisers, consulting one of the banned mediums at Endor. This was on the eve of the battle in which he died by his own hand.

At the end of his life Saul cuts a pathetic figure — lonely, discouraged, concerned about the future and turning to the agents of gods he had himself attempted to remove. In the battle between flesh and the spirit, the flesh had won. Saul was, finally, a man who fell prey to his own fears. Insecurity took him along a path away from God and from sanity.

THE DOWNWARD SPIRAL

King Saul's life is an instructive example of the debilitating effects of insecurity and the anxiety that results. The steps which led to the downward spiral, terminating in his departure from God's will, are often repeated today.

Consider these steps for a moment. To begin with, Saul's initial grasp of spiritual things was defective. From the start his spiritual awareness was low and his commitment to the Lord incomplete. There was in Saul a struggle between the natural and the supernatural. Apparently he never felt completely comfortable with the supernatural realm. The consequence was that, even after God had changed his heart and empowered him by the Spirit, he still had a tendency to revert to natural ways of reasoning and to his own natural abilities.

After an initial foray against the Ammonites when he successfully relied upon the divine initiative Saul slid back into his own pattern of thinking by degrees. As a result he was not secure in God and his consequent inability to hear clearly from God led him to seek security in other people's opinions. He constantly courted popularity, unaware that popularity-seeking inevitably dulls spiritual sensitivity. His inability to trust Samuel, God's servant, and therefore to trust God himself, developed out of uncertainty as to whether Samuel could be relied upon, in spite of the fact that, from previous experience, he had every reason to trust the prophet. Insecurity which seeks buttressing from the majority vote takes no notice of relevant facts. Popular opinion is a poor guide when it comes to spiritual realities.

Once established, Saul's habit of leaning on the good

opinion of others led not to security but into disobedience to God. Putting up a facade of acceptability before the leaders of his people was more important than facing up to God's assessment.

If he had responded sincerely to God's judgement by rejecting the fake basis of his hopes born of insecurity, things might have been different. As it was, Saul's fear of public failure resulted in paralyzing anxiety before Goliath. When a young man showed the way out of the morass through trust in God, Saul's response was to become jealous. He could not see beyond David's popularity to the underlying cause. David did not seek popularity, he sought to vindicate God. Because he could not grasp this fundamental principle, Saul only saw, and feared, his own personal eclipse.

Putting up a facade of acceptability before the leaders of his people was more important than facing up to God's assessment.

By this time Saul was unable to distinguish between reality and appearances. His jealousy fuelled his depression, driving him mad. He lost the support of God, Samuel, the people and his own son. In desperation he turned to spiritism for reassurance. Even this offered no hope for his insecurity. Finally, he committed suicide on the battle-field, terrified lest the enemy should taunt and abuse him. To the end Saul relied on natural solutions to his problems rather than trust God.

NATURAL SOLUTIONS

To employ natural solutions in the resolution of spiritual problems is to court disaster. God is not confronted with problems, only opportunities. The word 'problem' is never once used in the Bible.

Saul was provided with both the natural and spiritual equipment to complete the task to which he had been called. But his sense of inferiority led to insecurity. This, in turn, caused him increasingly to rely on natural solutions when the supernatural was available. Insecurity is a species of anxiety. As with Saul, anxiety frequently turned our God-given calling and equipping into animosity. Those united with us and working alongside us, in the spiritual battle are falsely identified as a threat, and we behave inappropriately towards them to relieve the pressure of that threat.

Indeed, natural solutions to spiritual challenges are always inappropriate. We are reminded of the student taking his final examinations. He felt insecure in his preparation and was terrified of the prospect of the exam. His solution was to take amphetymines before going into the examination hall. Other candidates were impressed with the confidence with which he sat down to write and the frequency with which he requested fresh sheets of paper. About half an hour before the end of the session the effects of the capsules began to wear off. He looked down at what he had written only to discover that for 2.5 hours he had been signing his name over and over again!

There was another Benjaminite, also named Saul, who took inappropriate action to solve spiritual issues. Thinking he was helping God out, he persecuted the early Christians. It took his personal Damascus road experience to change the perspective. Divinely appointed and anointed to be a light to the Gentiles, he became the greatest missionary of all time. In the process his name was changed to Paul.

This change of name represents a change of character. In his letter to the Galatians, he upbraids the Jewish Christians who were demanding that Gentiles obey Jewish laws to be right with God. Paul reveals the secret of a life freed from anxiety. 'I have been crucified with Christ,' he says, 'and I no longer live, but Christ lives in me. The life I live in the body, I live by faith in the Son of God' (Galatians 2:20). No room for insecurity there.

Paul had learned not to rely on the good opinion of others for his security; even of the most revered apostles. He knew who he was in Christ.

An American Airline stewardess on an international flight was treated badly by a first-class passenger who behaved overbearingly and rudely towards her. His behaviour was abrupt, his language harsh and his attitude unkind. Throughout the flight she showed no signs of annoyance and she only responded calmly, courteously and with kindness.

Something got through to the passenger, obviously an important businessman. As he left the aeroplane at the termination of the flight the man singled the girl out. 'I will mention you to the chairman of the company,' he said. The girl, who was a Christian, retorted, 'That's all right, sir. I work to please another!'

PART
4

DELIVERANCE

How To Deal With Anxiety

7

Causes and Cure

A nxiety is a spiritual disease. When you have a disease it is normal to find a specialist who can diagnose it and treat it. This is what we need to do with anxiety. *More anxiety will not deliver us!* People who are prone to excessive anxiety need delivering from it. So far we have looked at both the symptoms of, and the reasons for, anxiety. Implicit in all we have said is the fact that the root cause of excessive anxiety is sin — and sin arises when we fail to focus on God.

ITS CAUSES

Anxiety is basically a virulent form of self-centredness, of looking towards ourselves, and not looking towards God. This is not to suggest that we need to take no notice of our own selves. But there is the world of difference between a proper self-regard and the type of self-centred focus which results in unhealthy anxiety. The New Testament has a word for this kind of activity. Paul calls it 'the flesh'. By this he means not just our physical body but rather what results when our physical nature becomes locked in on itself. 'The flesh', in Paul's sense of the word, refers to the whole of our personality when it is dominated by the merely physical. It includes self-indulgent thoughts, emotions and desires. We could say that 'the flesh' stands for human nature when it is going in the wrong direction. It is what happens to a personality which is organized without reference to God. The flesh is the way we act when we excuse our conduct by saying, 'I'm only human, after all!' Anxiety is one of the 'works of the flesh', although it is not specifically listed as such in the Bible.

In order to deal with excessive anxiety it is necessary to admit frankly that undue anxiety arises as a consequence of sin.

ITS CURE

If sin is the root cause of anxiety then the answer to it must be salvation — found only in the saving power of Jesus. But this is where, for a Christian, a defective understanding of salvation can complicate the problem. If we see salvation as a once and for all event in the past, and equate it with our conversion, to be told that anxiety is a sin makes us feel guilty, condemned and even more anxious! The truth is that the Bible tells us that the message of the Cross is the power of God to those of us who are *in the process of being saved* (1 Corinthians 1:18, NIV). When Paul tells the Philippian believers to outwork their salvation with fear and trembling, knowing that God is at work in us so that we can desire and do that he wants to do (Philippians 2:12 – 13), we can conclude that there is a process to go through. In other words, salvation *begins* with an event in our lives based on what Jesus did on the cross, but the consequences of this event have *continually* to be worked through in our lives.

Salvation is not just forgiveness from sin but much more.

Its root meaning is 'wholeness'. In the New Testament, the word 'salvation' is primarily used in a sense borrowed from classical Greek.

> ...'to save' is connected with salvation in the sense of health: it means to restore health to one who has lost it, to restore safety to one who is threatened by a danger, to snatch from death someone who is about to perish...it should be noted above all that here Jesus often appears as the author of this immediate and tangible act of deliverance. He saves the disciples from the storm, He rescues Peter from drowning; and in parallel circumstances He does not save himself from the cross. The fact is that the New Testament does not distinguish between a spiritual salvation of the soul and a salvation which might be considered less important, of the body. It envisages the person as a whole and considers that a sick or drowning man is totally threatened and that such a one would not hesitate to invoke the name of Jesus.
>
> *P. Bonnard*, Vocabulary of the Bible, *ed. J – J. Allmon.*

Of course this kind of salvation is a pointer to a complete salvation. There is a group of New Testament passages where Bonnard notes that: 'Salvation is no longer understood as a particular or provisional deliverance but as a total and ultimate deliverance.' The point is that:

> Salvation in the New Testament is always understood as a deliverance or a liberation, not as an accession to a higher or more spiritual life. The transition from the state of a man lost or enslaved to that of a man in a state of grace is not affected by a process of development ... but as the result of a sharp break, a reversal of values, a death through which salvation is achieved.

Where does this leave us? Salvation is deliverance to a state of wholeness, whether that means wholeness in relation to a specific situation or in relation to our total experience. Just as salvation in a particular area of life points to complete salvation, so the potentially complete salvation has to be applied to the particular events of life.

In relation to anxiety, salvation is a deliverance from fear, doubt and worry. Because anxiety is a consequence of sin and itself becomes sinful, we need to be saved from both the sin and its consequences. Anxiety can and does arise from all sorts of pressures. Whether it becomes sinful or not depends on how we handle it. Justified concern can result in either condemnation or conquest, depending on what we do with it. To take an example from Paul. In his second letter to the Corinthian believers he reports the hardship he and his team of men suffered in the province of Asia. 'We were under great pressure, far beyond our ability to endure, so that we despaired even of life. Indeed, in our hearts we felt the sentence of death.' Here was real cause for anxiety, but how did Paul and his party deal with it? 'But this happened that we might not rely upon ourselves but on God, who raises the dead. He has delivered us from such a deadly peril, and he will deliver us. On him we have set our hope that he will continue to deliver us' (2 Corinthians 1:9 – 10).

Note the words 'continue to'. The hope is to be delivered from physical danger. Evidently the cross and the resurrection provide a hope that delivers people in situations that are physical, earthly pressures, not just 'spiritual' problems. The clue is to rely not on ourselves but on God.

STEPS TO DELIVERANCE

The good news is that there is a cure for anxiety. In order for it to be dealt with there is a process which must be followed. That process can be seen as three steps in our salvation, steps which lead to wholeness. These steps can be called recognition, redemption and restoration. Let us briefly look at each one.

• **Recognition.** Recognize anxiety for what it is. Physical symptoms brought on by tension can be ignored, misinterpreted or simply brushed aside. In order to cure these they must be seen for what they are — the fruits of anxiety. And the excessive anxiety which produces these symptoms must be identified for what it is — sin. For excessive anxiety advertizes a lack of trust in God and his ability to deal with our circumstances. In addition, anxiety makes us more and more self-centred, and so negative feelings become the measure of everything that we do. Anxiety draws our attention persistently in upon ourselves. This is the very nature of sin and is the reversal of God's values for our lives.

• **Redemption.** Recognition of the problem alone can compound it. If we see clearly that anxiety is sinful, that in itself will cause more anxiety unless the sin-root is dealt with. So the next step is to secure redemption, for the sin of anxiety is covered by the victory which Jesus won for us on the cross. We read in Ephesians 1:7 – 8, 'In him we have redemption through his blood, the forgiveness of sins.' Not only this, our forgiveness is 'in accordance with the riches of God's grace that he lavished on us with all wisdom and understanding.' Whatever else it means, Paul explains here that redemption is the 'forgiveness of sins'. In order to be redeemed from anxiety, we need to ask forgiveness. So often anxiety-sufferers ask God to deal with the occasion for the anxiety, or even with the anxiety itself, but seldom do they confess it as a sin and ask his forgiveness for it.

Among other things, redemption means 'to buy back'. It was used in the Old Testament to indicate what happened when a kinsman avenged a wrong done to, or paid the

penalty of an offence committed by, a person. Part of the
'Statute of Limitations' of Old Testament law was that only
the nearest kinsman could perform this function. By his
birth into humanity and by his death for humanity, Jesus is
our nearest kinsman. He performs the functions of avenging
the wrongs perpetrated by anxiety and of paying the penalty
incurred by the anxious.

In order to be redeemed from anxiety, we need to ask forgiveness.

In the Roman and Greek worlds of the New Testament
era, redemption was a term to cover the process of buying
and freeing a slave. When we find ourselves in the slave
market of sin, only Jesus can buy us back from the slave-
master of anxiety. Therefore only he can set us free. In the
Old Testament the psalmists grappled with the problem of
redemption. One of them records, 'No man can redeem the
life of another or give to God a ransom for him — the ransom for a life is costly, no payment is ever enough' (Psalm
49:7 – 8, NIV). The realization in verse 15: 'But God will
redeem my life from the grave; he will surely take me to
himself', is a different perspective. It takes a New Testament
perspective to realize that we need Jesus, the God-Man, to
redeem us from the grave of the anxiety that threatens to
overwhelm and bury us.

• **Restoration.** Even redemption is insufficient on its own.
For our deliverance to be complete we must avoid return-
ing to old battlefields. We have a choice; live in victory, or
despair in the graveyard of forgiven sin. Too often we spend
our time exhuming the corpses of past defeat!

We need to progress beyond redemption to restoration.
We are bought with a price, not only to be freed tempor-

arily but to enter into the privileges of sonship. This means we can exercise our freedom continually. We have already noted that when Jesus redeemed us it was not in small measure but in accordance with the riches God lavished upon us, the riches of his grace. I like the word 'lavished', it is expansive, it indicates that God has done for us even more than we need. The letter to the Ephesians tells us that this grace was poured out on us with all wisdom and understanding. That means that, together with his unmerited love which buys us back from sin, God also gave us gifts of wisdom and understanding so that we can stay bought. We can remain in his purposes, restored to his full intention for us. We need not return to our sinful state. That covers anxiety, as well as every other sin.

THE PATTERN OF SALVATION

It is this simple pattern of salvation that needs to be applied to our lives, at deeper and deeper levels. We need to grow into maturity and deeper into holiness. The pattern of salvation can be followed through as we get to know Jesus better. In the next few chapters we will consider:

- Love *from* the Father;
- The Lordship *of* Christ;
- Leadership *by* the Holy Spirit.

As we look at these areas they will help us to work out the pattern of salvation in relation to dealing with anxiety.

8

Love from the Father

Many anxiety-states involve distorted views of God as Father. It is amazing how frequently such twisted views of God find their root in a troubled relationship with a natural father or substitute father. There are children — and adults — with whom it is difficult to share the concept of the Fatherhood of God because their experience of a father is a menacing or fearful one. A child who has been battered in infancy and early childhood by a brutal man simply cannot relate to the idea of God's fathering.

But sometimes the distortion caused by an earthly father is far more subtle and less obvious than this. Even when a parent intends the best for his child, the wrong message may be conveyed. The sources of this often lie in the parents' background and so the shortcomings of the fathers are passed on from one generation to another.

To take an example, Wanda's father cared for her and desperately wanted the best for her. He had himself been through a hard upbringing. Life had not been easy for his hard-working folk during the years of the depression and consequently he saw security in terms of financial success.

He dearly wanted his daughter to succeed in a career and to be secure. In order to drive her towards the goals which he had selected for her, he was over-strict. Throughout her childhood Wanda felt that she could not match her father's expectations. When she did well he always expected her to do better. Though he praised her abilities in her absence he never encouraged her personally. Wanda grew up afraid of making decisions. She developed an inability to share either her successes or her failings in case she would be put down. At the same time she was always anxious to gain acceptance and recognition. She became a secretive but anxious striver. As a result of this, her view of God was of a tyrant who could never be satisfied, and so she was never totally sure of her standing with him. Confidence in God's care for her became a victim of her anxiety in which she imagined an exacting God whose standards she could never meet.

Bad fathering can lead to a false division between our view of God the Father and God the Son.

David, in contrast, was one of three children whose father was relatively indulgent to them all. Nevertheless, his younger brother, Nigel, was their dad's favourite. He always got the extra candy bar, more cuddles and greater acceptance. David received love too, but it always seemed to him that he was pushed on to the sidelines when Nigel was around. He was able to relate to his brother, who was a lovable character, but with some reserve. It is hardly surprising that when David eventually became a Christian he developed an unconscious view of God as someone who was fickle and capricious. He was never sure that God could be relied upon and although he believed in God's love it seemed that other Christians were honoured and blessed more than he was. In childhood he had learned to compare blessings to his own detriment.

These are only two illustrations out of many. An over-indulgent father can rear children who develop a 'Father Christmas' view of God. When their expectations of fatherly goodies are not fulfilled, a high degree of anxiety is generated which can lead to spiritual depression. At the other extreme, an unrewarding father may produce a striving child, and an unrelenting earthly father will nurture a sense of failure in his children. All too often these inbuilt distortions of fatherhood are carried over into a person's view of God. Even a life-changing experience of Christ does not always correct this false image of God the Father. This is why many people confess that they find it easier to relate to Jesus than to the thought of God as a heavenly Father.

Bad fathering can lead to a false division between our view of God the Father and God the Son. The biblical reality is that it was the Father who in his concern for us, sent his only begotten Son to show his true nature towards us. Jesus came to reveal the 'father-heart' of God. It is he, more than anyone else, who fixed the concept of the Fatherhood of God into man's consciousness. The idea of God as our Father was not unique to Jesus but he was the one who made it real. He fleshed the concept of Fatherhood by his own response as a Son. The continental scholar, Mehl, remarks, 'The Old Testament taught that God is the Living God and a Father. The New Testament teaches us the meaning to attach to these statements' (*Vocabulary of the Bible*, p 149). The letter to the Hebrews reminds us:

> In bringing many sons to glory it was fitting that God, for whom and through whom everything exists, should make the author of their salvation perfect [mature] through suffering. Both the one who makes men holy

and those who are made holy are of the same family. So Jesus is not ashamed to call them brothers.

Hebrews 2:10 – 11, NIV

There is no dichotomy: the Father is the same to us as Jesus is and, moreover, he treated Jesus in the same way he treats us — he makes us mature through suffering.

What God the Father has done for us in giving salvation through Christ shows his real attitude towards us. This on its own should cause us to let go of our anxiety.

THE FATHER'S NATURE

In his letter to the Ephesians the apostle Paul reminds us that as Christians our family name comes from God the Father. We are meant to be united under a family crest which describes Father's nature or character. Paul says: 'I kneel before the Father from whom the whole family in heaven and on earth derives its name' (Ephesians 3:14 – 15, NIV). Moffatt's translation says, 'from whom every family in heaven and on earth derives its name and nature.'

Clearly not every human family, not even every Christian family, is made in the mould which God intends for it. There are brutal fathers and neglectful mothers. However, the essential nature of family relationships expresses God's purpose for us: he is a God who desires to be in relationship with us, as our Father. Although there is a sense in which God is both judge and general, his heart is that of a father and he desires to father us.

An alternative rendering of the verse above is found in the New International Version margin: 'I kneel before the Father from whom all *fatherhood* in heaven and on earth derives its name.' This is in keeping with the spirit of the passage. The point is that we are not to measure the quality of family life or our understanding of fatherhood by our own human experience. Rather, we are to pattern our family life, and our practice of fatherhood, on the example of God as our Father.

If our experience of family life serves to distort our view of God it will consequently lead to anxiety. The corrective is to base our view of family life on the example of God. We must get our view of proper human fathering from our knowledge of the Fatherhood of God. The hymn-writer Frederick Faber wrote:

> All Fathers learn their craft from thee:
> All loves are shadows cast
> From the beautiful eternal hills
> Of Thine unbeginning past.

However good it may have been, we must never derive our view of God's fathering from an inadequate human model.

THE REVELATION OF FATHER

If we are to be secure in the father-love of God we need to understand that love more clearly and more biblically.

But how are we to get at the biblical revelation of the Fatherhood of God? There are two ways in which we can go about it which are equally sound. The first of these is historical and the second is psychological. Of these the psychological is perhaps the most rewarding but let us look at them both in turn.

The Old Testament

The first picture we get of God in the Bible is of a Creator who made the earth and gave it into the hands of human beings to tend. He appears as a friend but nevertheless as a ruler and a judge, against whom man rebels. From then on, God is seen as the one who intervenes at crucial points in history, although he is also portrayed as the one without whom the human story could not take place. The Old Testament revelation of the Fatherhood of God hinges upon these two facts — creation and intervention. The term 'father' is used sparingly in the Old Testament in relation to God.

Wherever the term 'father' is used, the primary reference is as a 'father' to Israel as a nation. This differs considerably from the New Testament view, as we will see later. It seems that the Bible authors had God's creator-relationship with Israel in mind more than his relationship with all people. For instance, in Deuteronomy 32, verse 6, Moses asks, 'Is this the way you repay the Lord, O foolish and unwise people? Is he not your Father, your Creator who made and formed you?' He goes on to speak of the nations, but the real focus is stated in verse 9, 'For the Lord's portion is his people, Jacob his allotted inheritance.' While it is true that the generalized Fatherhood of God is a corollary of the creature-hood of man, nevertheless, the primary focus in the Old Testament, even when speaking of the Creator, is upon the nation of Israel.

This closely relates to the second strand of Old Testament thinking: the God who intervenes decisively at particular points in history. These interventions usually relate to his choice of Israel as a nation and the covenant he made with them. Thus, his Fatherhood is always a moral relationship. For example, Psalm 68, verse 5, says, 'A father to the father-less, a defender of widows, is God in his holy dwelling.' And verse 6 continues, 'he sets the lonely in families'. The Lord does this to fulfil his covenant with Israel, he is the Father of the nation because he has redeemed it. Even the Lord's judgement of Israel is explained in terms of his parental function to them: 'The Lord saw this and rejected them because he was angered by his sons and daughters' (Deuteronomy 32:19). In the ancient world a father had absolute and unlimited rights over his children. This was true of God's relationship with Israel.

In chapter 63 of Isaiah, the prophet appeals to the tenderness of God towards the nation precisely because God had redeemed them:

> Look down from heaven and see from your lofty throne, holy and glorious. Where are your zeal and your might? Your tenderness and compassion are withheld from us. But you are our Father, though Abraham does not know us or Israel acknowledge us; you, O Lord, are our Father, our Redeemer from of old is your name.

There could be no clearer statement of the connection between God's function as a father and his favour as a redeemer. For Israel, God's Fatherhood was of grace. It was *the* covenant blessing. Nevertheless, it was not an individualized fatherhood. The Nation was the Son, not the individuals who composed it. This is different from the New Testament, where we become members of God's new nation by individual birth. In the Old Testament birthright came from belonging to the group; under the new covenant we become members of the group by receiving birth.

The New Covenant

The Old Testament gives one hint of the individual birth pattern which was to come. God had a unique Son, prefigured by King David, who nevertheless became recognized in his Sonship through obedience. Psalm 2 says of the King who he has installed upon his holy hill of Zion, 'You are my son, today I have become your Father.' We may be right to hear an echo of this in God's statement over Jesus at his baptism. Whatever else it indicates, Psalm 2 establishes a direct connection between Sonship and Kingship. God's Son came to reign and his children are called to rule with him.

Jesus revealed the personalized Fatherhood of God. He

recognized that God created us but he also taught that, by an act of faith, his Father could become the Father of each one of us. That act of faith centres around our attitude to God's unique Son, Jesus. This is why the apostle John wrote about him:

> He was in the world, and though the world was made through him, the world did not recognise him. He came to that which was his own, but his own did not receive him. Yet to all who received him, to those who believed in his name, he gave the right to become children of God — children born not of natural descent, nor of human decision or a husband's will, but born of God.
>
> *John 1:10 – 13*

Our Sonship depends simply upon the reception we give to Jesus. Having received Jesus, God's Fatherhood comes into play. His care and concern becomes operative towards us, not for the first time, because he always cared for us, but in a new dimension. We enter his household and become his particular care. That is why we can take hold of the Bible's invitation, and command, to cast our cares upon him, because he cares constantly for us as a father.

Consideration of this should calm our fears and quell our anxieties.

'Our Father'

In summary, God's Fatherhood is not based primarily upon his creative activity but upon his redemptive act. Not everybody is qualified to pray, 'Our Father'. The bringing to birth of the nation Israel, by the redemptive events of deliverance from Egypt, is paralleled in the New Testament by the decisive act of Jesus on the cross.

Just as the individual Israelite came into a covenant blessing by physical birth into the nation, we came into a relationship of Sonship to God by a faith which brings about spiritual birth. This birth brings us into God's family. To belong to his family means both that God has absolute rights over us and that he cares for us.

When he is our Father, God plans good things for us so we have nothing to fear. The nation of Israel knew prosperity and blessing when they remained in faithful covenant relationship with God. Just so, we can be assured that as long as we depend upon him, he will deal with our anxieties and relieve us of our fears.

CONSCIOUSNESS OF SONSHIP

Our understanding of sonship can also be approached from a psychological standpoint. To get the best insight into our relationship with God as Father, we need to turn to Jesus. Because of his unique relationship, Jesus reveals to us most clearly the Father-heart of God. These insights come not so much from the direct teaching which Jesus gave on this subject, as from his consciousness of God revealed by incidental statements. The psychology of sonship is shown in the way in which Jesus handled situations and referred them to the Father. Nowhere is this more true than in John's portrait of the Christ in his Gospel. However, it occurs in the other Gospels too.

No one's outward circumstances potentially gave rise to anxiety more than those of Jesus. From early on in his public ministry he was under constant attack from Satan, opposition from the religious leaders, suspicion from the political establishment and misunderstanding from his family and supporters. Nowhere in the Gospels does Jesus show any signs of undue anxiety about the pressures which surround him. This is because he was secure in his Father's love. He was, from the age of twelve, aware that God has a special purpose for his life. He moved in the security of finding his Father's will and doing it.

When he was stranded in the temple precincts at the age of twelve Jesus showed no signs of concern that he was temporarily cut off from his earthly parents. They exhibited first carelessness and then extreme concern that the boy was lost to them for three days. When they finally found him in the temple courtyards, listening to the teachers and asking questions, they were astonished, relieved and, probably, annoyed. Mary, displaying a mother's heart, chided him, 'Son, why have you treated us like this? Your father and I have been anxiously searching for you.' Luke records the boy's answer. It was not born of impudence but the serenity of certainty. 'Why were you searching for me?' he asked. 'Didn't you know I had to be in my Father's house?'

It is recorded that Mary and Joseph did not understand. Why didn't he want to come home with them? There was a real sense in which the young lad *had* come home. He had found his fulfilment in his Father's house. Some versions of the Bible render this question, 'Did you not know I had to be about my Father's business?' There is a genuine insight here. Although 'my Father's house' refers firstly to the Temple, the deeper sense is that Jesus was in his Father's 'household'. Therefore he was doing Father's business. Jesus never showed any sign of being tied to particular religious places. His consciousness of God was rooted in knowing where he belonged in God's will, irrespective of the specific location. Jesus never lost that sense of being in his Father's house. That is why, much later, he was able to say, 'In my Father's house are many rooms...I am going there to prepare a place for you' (John 14:2).

Affirmation

At the beginning of his public ministry this consciousness of being in God's will was confirmed. As Jesus was baptized in water, identifying himself with the sins of the people, the Holy Spirit descended upon him. In full public view God's voice from heaven said, 'This is my Son, whom I love; with him I am well pleased' (Matthew 3:17).

This was not the only occasion when God publicly affirmed this inner certainty which Jesus enjoyed. At the point when the disciples were truly beginning to recognize who he was, not only in name, Jesus took three of them up a mountain. In the Transfiguration, Jesus was glorified before them, confirming Peter's earlier claim, 'You are the Christ the Son of the living God' (Matthew 16:16). Yet, as Jesus talked with Moses and Elijah who had appeared to them, Peter backed down on his earlier revelation. 'Rabbi,' he said, 'Let us put up three booths [shrines] — one for you, one for Moses and one for Elijah' (Mark 9:5). In other words, 'Let us revere you on a level with these two great teachers?' God intervened first by enveloping them with a cloud, obscuring Moses and Elijah. Then, by saying, 'This is my Son, whom I love. Listen to him!' God was pointing both to the uniqueness of the ministry of Jesus and of his relationship to the Father.

Potential anxiety

The Transfiguration marked an important new development in the life of Jesus. It was a time of potential anxiety. Jesus was beginning to face up to going to Jerusalem to die. He had also begun to prepare his disciples by teaching them about the need for him to die and be raised again. They had demonstrated a new stage of awareness, but were they ready to cope with this? God the Father underwrote what

Jesus was saying by his intervention on the Mount of Transfiguration.

Another such crisis came when Jesus began to teach publicly about his impending death. According to John's Gospel, the trigger for this new development was when Philip and Andrew brought some Greeks who wanted to see Jesus. This opening up of God's message to the Gentiles is significant for Jesus' ministry to the whole world, but that universal opportunity would only be brought about fully by his death, resurrection, ascension and Pentecost. Jesus saw clearly that he was about to achieve glory and that for him it would mean the seed-corn loneliness of the grave.

The prospect was daunting, but Jesus did not give way to anxiety. He honestly admitted, 'Now my heart is troubled, and what shall I say? "Father save me from this hour? No; it was for this very reason I came to this hour." Father, glorify your name!'

The response was immediate, 'Then a voice came from heaven, "I have glorified it, and will glorify it again"' (John 12:28). God publicly endorsed what Jesus experienced in his heart. His sense of what Father was saying was upheld in front of the bystanders.

The basis of relationship

From the beginning of his ministry Jesus was subjected to intense pressures. After his baptism he was driven into the desert by the Holy Spirit. There he went through severe testing, not only from physical hunger but also from spiritual questioning (see Matthew 4:1 – 11). He had been commissioned by God, but what was to be the nature of his ministry?

The anxiety of uncertainty could have left Jesus undecided and impotent. He was being tested along the line of his willingness to follow his Father's programme. Satan attempted to deter him by attacking his sense of Sonship. Three times he insinuated, 'If you are the Son of God...'. Satan's taunt to Jesus was, 'If you have had this experience, prove it.' The response of Jesus is revealing. Firstly, his Sonship did not depend upon his earthly physical life but on observing 'every word coming from the mouth of God.' Secondly, Jesus knew that to act outside of the right way to live in God was to test God unduly. Satan misquoted Psalm 91: it does indeed say that God would command his angels to lift you up so that you will not strike your foot against a stone, but he cleverly missed out the linking clause — 'to guard you in all your ways'. 'All your ways' carries a qualification with it. Earlier the psalmist had said, 'If you make the Most High your dwelling — even the Lord, who is my refuge — then no harm will befall you.'

Satan attempted to deter him by attacking his sense of Sonship.

Thirdly, Jesus recognized that his relationship with God was to be based on worship and service rather than upon domination of men.

Jesus resisted the pressures and clung on to his relationship with his Father by basing his life on the principles outlined in Scripture. Satan said, 'If you are the Son of God.' Jesus did not permit doubt, nor did he base his response upon an appeal to past experience; even the recent past. His consciousness of the Father depended upon *present* obedience.

No wonder that Luke records, following this event, 'Jesus returned to Galilee in the power of the Spirit' (Luke 4:14). He went into the desert *full* of the Spirit but he returned, after the trial over his sonship, *in the power* of the Spirit.

Frank recognition

A further crisis came for Jesus after John the Baptist was arrested. John began to doubt whether he had rightly discerned that Jesus was the coming Messiah. From prison he sent a message which was not exactly calculated to bolster Jesus' confidence! 'Are you the one who was to come or should we expect someone else?' John may be paraphrased as saying, 'Here am I in prison and I don't understand what you are up to out there. Whatever you think you are doing, this isn't what I expected. Please reassure me.'

Jesus simply told the messengers to go back and report what they heard and saw, 'The blind receive sight, the lame walk, those who have leprosy are cured, the deaf hear, the dead are raised, and the good news is preached to the poor.' This may not have been the form of the Kingdom which John was expecting, but was it not better? Jesus ended his reply with a word of encouragement to John: 'Blessed is the man who does not fall away on account of me' (Matthew 11:2 – 7).

After commending John before the crowds for his uncompromising stand, Jesus condemned the unbelief of the cynical cities in which he had himself ministered. John's warnings of doom would indeed fall upon *them*.

Here then was Jesus, doubted by John, the man of God who had launched him on his ministry and rejected by the over-privileged godless to whom he ministered. He could have been tempted to despair. Instead, he calmly looked up to heaven and said, 'I praise you, Father, Lord of heaven and earth, because you have hidden these things from the wise and learned, and revealed them to little children. Yes, Father, for this was your good pleasure' (Matthew 11:25 – 26).

Jesus frankly recognized who his Father was, the Lord of

heaven and earth. Consequently, everything was under control and he, the Son, had no need to worry.

The statement which follows in verse 27 is so uncharacteristic of the first three Gospels that one scholar has described it as a bolt from the heavens of John's Gospel! 'All things have been committed to me by my Father. No one knows the Son except the Father, and no one knows the Father except the Son and those to whom the Son chooses to reveal him.' This is consistent with Jesus' statement recorded in John's Gospel where he is reported as saying that he only spoke what he heard from the Father and he only did what he saw his Father doing (John 5:19; 8:28). Indeed, when he healed the paralyzed man at the pool of Bethesda and subsequently dealt with his sins, Jesus justified himself by implying that he was completing the creative work of God who was his Father.

THE AWARENESS OF JESUS

There is much more that can be said about Jesus' consciousness of his Father. It is a big subject. Although it is true that the relationship of Jesus to the Father is unique, ours has strong parallels. We too are sons of the Father. He always was, we had to become, his sons by faith. But what can we glean about the Father-love of God from the awareness of Jesus?

As Jesus saw and experienced Sonship, God affirmed and publicly supported him. He always lived in the Father's household under his domination, tested and disciplined, but always kept and sustained by him. Jesus was conscious of the Father's care. His Father is a King who, if we are committed to him and his Kingdom, never fails to provide us with everything we need. Therefore, there is no need to be anxious about the future.

That was true for Jesus as much as it is for us. God required difficult things of Jesus but he consistently provided the inner resources to see them through to their conclusion. Because of this Jesus knew not to worry.

In his book, *Vision and Authority*, John Oman comments:

> If all that is spent on worry were spent on toil, if all pain of anticipation were pains of concentration, if all dismay at ills that never came and shrinking from blows that never fall were spent in the energy of present diligence, the claims of the day, though sufficient, would never be over-whelming. The error is not in the anxiety, but in the waste of a commodity so precious. To be anxious for the morrow is to take our care from where it is urgently needed, to bestow it where it is unavailing. And every time we thus misapply our diligence, the need for peering anxiously into the future seems to increase.

Jesus practised that concentration of energy which rested secure in the provision and purpose of a Father who was Lord of heaven and earth, the King in his Kingdom. The knowledge of the Fatherhood of God is an antidote to anxiety because that knowledge is rooted in who he is.

9

The Lordship of the Son

As a new, inexperienced teacher, Dick explains, I took up my first appointment in London's East End. It was at a time when anyone with a degree could enter the teaching profession without further training or teaching qualifications.

So there I was, with a degree, no experience and no training, working in a tough school in a hard area of the city. The teenagers I taught were aggressive, noisy, and equipped with street-wise shrewdness and typical quick Cockney humour. The school, in a poor area, was under-equipped and the Headmaster was coasting to retirement. He was a former player for one of London's first division football teams and he bathed in the reflected glow of their current success. The Head seemed blissfully unaware that his staff were experiencing difficulties. Even when members of staff were physically assaulted in the corridor or the classroom, he made excuses.

Looking back, I suppose that I didn't do too badly in the circumstances. But I have vivid memories of one class of teenagers refusing to co-operate as the boys stood on their desks and jeered and the girls laughed. If it hadn't been for the Deputy Head I would never have survived. I remember regularly travelling home, a long journey on the London Underground system, white and drained from the strain. It was a baptism of fire. Anxiety was high and a recurring nightmare was of classes of large teenagers rioting. By the grace of God I survived and went on to a career in education which took me into an eventual position of teaching others to teach — I think I had something to impart which went beyond the realms of theory!

The point of this story is that anxiety is always heightened when we are underprivileged, underpowered or underprepared. I was all three, so you can imagine the levels of anxiety which almost gave way to nervous exhaustion.

Even in these circumstances, anxiety can be overcome if someone else is responsible. I would not have survived in that school if it had not been for a strong and kindly Deputy Head who took the responsibility. The good news is that, if we will let him, Jesus takes responsibility in our lives.

POWER AND AUTHORITY

At the start of my teaching career the basic problem was that I lacked the power to do the job. At some time in their experience most Christians feel like this about their commitment to Christ. Instead of being an answer to anxiety, their Christian profession becomes a further source of anxiety because they feel that they are underpowered. It becomes one more dimension of failure in their lives.

The New Testament distinguishes two kinds of power. The first is expressed by the Greek word *dunamis* which basically means 'power' or 'ability'. After his testing in the wilderness we read that 'Jesus returned in the *dunamis* of the Spirit.' The good news of gospel is described as the 'power [or ability] of God for Salvation' (Romans 1:16). The disciples were told that if they waited in Jerusalem they would receive *dunamis* after the Holy Spirit had come upon them and Paul describes Jesus as 'the power of God and the Wisdom of God' (1 Corinthians 1:24). *Dunamis* is, briefly, the power or ability to get the job done and Scripture teaches not only that Jesus has that power but that he *is* the power we need.

Jesus never fails to give the power and authority to those willing to take it up.

The second New Testament word for power is *exousia*, which means the power of privilege or authority. Jesus began his earthly ministry by announcing that 'the Son of Man has authority on earth to forgive sins' (Mark 2:10) and he proved it by healing a paralyzed man who was in sin. Right at the end of his ministry Jesus left his disciples with a mandate and the backing to fulfil it, 'All authority in heaven and earth has been given to me,' he said, 'therefore go and make disciples of all nations.' As an old Bible teacher of mine used to say, 'When the Bible says "therefore" you have to ask what it is there for!' In this case the 'therefore' indicates that we are to go *precisely* because Jesus has all the authority needed to send us effectively.

We can obey and succeed in this task because *he* has the authority. It is a fundamental tenet of modern management theory that you do not give an employee any responsibility without first giving him appropriate authority. I ended the prefect system in one of the schools for which I was responsible. My reasoning was that too few senior students wanted the job anyway and, moreover, the other students refused to recognize the authority given to the prefects by the staff. Wearing the badge doesn't make you a Sheriff! Jesus never fails to give the power and authority to those willing to take it up.

THE NATURE OF AUTHORITY

Jesus was not often taken by surprise but one man managed to stop him in his tracks. After the Roman Centurion asked Jesus just to speak the word and his servant would be healed at a distance, we read,

> When Jesus heard this, he was astonished and said to those following him, 'I tell you the truth, I have not found anyone in Israel with such great faith. I say to you that many will come from the east and the west, and will take their places at the feast with Abraham, Isaac and Jacob in the Kingdom of Heaven.'
>
> *Matthew 8:10 – 11*

What was it that pleased Jesus so much about the faith of this Gentile seeker after truth? It wasn't the fact that the Centurion believed that Jesus was not limited in his power by distance. It was the reason which the man gave for his conviction about Jesus that impressed, for the Centurion explained, 'Lord I do not deserve to have you come under my roof. But just say the word, and my servant will be healed. For I myself am a man under authority. I tell this one, "Go" and he goes; and that one, "Come" and he comes. I say to my servant, "Do this", and he does it' (verses 8 – 9). In other words, the man not only recognized the authority of Jesus but he discerned the source of that authority.

The Centurion said, 'I myself am a man under authority.' The Authorized Version helpfully translates it as, 'I *too* am a man under authority.' He recognized that he and Jesus were in a similar situation, for they both wielded a derived authority. As a Centurion, men obeyed him not because of who he was but because the stars on his shoulder indicated that he spoke with the authority, and consequently all the backing of power, of the Emperor and the Senate in Rome. Jesus wields the authority of his Father, the Emperor of Heaven.

Furthermore, the Centurion put his finger on the qualification to exercise the authority vested in him by Rome. 'I too am a man *under* authority.' It is only those who know how to submit to authority who can responsibly exercise authority. This is a spiritual principle.

In the Kingdom of God authority is a privilege (*exousia*) but it is never a matter of status. If we look at Mark chapter 10, verse 35 onwards, we see that when two of his disciples were vying for position, Jesus called the whole group to order. The rest of the disciples protested the audacity of James and John but, doubtless, it was only because James and John were expressing what was in their own hearts. Jesus corrected them all. 'You know,' he said, 'that those who are regarded as rulers over the Gentiles lord it over them, and their high officials exercise authority over them. Not so with you. Instead, whoever wants to become great among you must be your servant, and whoever wants to be first must be slave of all.'

The way up is the way down! Not that we should aim to become servants in order to become leaders. God is not deceived by such a charade. Rather, it is that true leaders in the Kingdom have a servant-heart. They would serve, even if it never led to recognition.

Jesus continued, 'For even the Son of Man did not come to be served, but to serve, and to give his life as a ransom for many.' Servanthood and redemption go together. How appropriate that the most authoritative man who ever lived took to himself the lowliest title 'Son of Man' and ended up his ministry by tucking a towel around his waist and picking up a bowl to wash the dusty feet of his followers.

There is a self-forgetfulness about true greatness and true

authority. It requires such self-forgetfulness to take up the authority to banish anxiety.

GIVING HIM AUTHORITY

In the heyday of the Roman Empire a common greeting in the forum or the market place was 'Caesar is Lord'. It was a way of demonstrating that you were a loyal citizen, one of the crowd, a member of the strong ruling club.

For Christians, this was not on. Instead, one Christian greeting another would exclaim, 'Jesus is Lord'. The reply would be, 'He is Lord, indeed.' Christians knew where they stood in relation to the authority of Jesus. This did not mean that they totally rejected the authority of Rome. They were more loyal citizens than most. It did mean that they were committed to a higher authority.

It was just this fact that caused Christians so much trouble in the Roman Empire. The State permitted no prior loyalties. In the days when Emperor worship was a test of trustworthiness, it was all right to have other gods as long as they did not challenge Caesar. 'After all,' popular thinking went, 'what is so difficult in offering a pinch of incense before Caesar's statue?'

But, just as the Emperor would allow no higher authority, neither would Jesus. The word 'Lord' means controller, master — something like our word 'boss'. And, as Jesus himself had said, in paraphrase, 'no man can have two bosses'. Christians were eager to render to Caesar that which was Caesar's, but first God must be given what was his. Where there was a conflict of claims between the two authorities, for the first Christians there was no contest.

The problem still remains for Christians today. It is only that in the so-called 'free world' the pressure is more subtle and the allegiance less obvious. This makes compromise so

much easier. However, the truth is that there is no alternative: either Jesus is Lord *of* all or he is not Lord *at* all. The
question remains: 'Who is the boss of your life?'

Unless we give Jesus the authority over our lives, we will
never be at peace. The anxiety which comes from dividing
our time between opposing ownerships can only be
resolved when we opt out and out for Jesus. The Bible calls
him Lord as well as Saviour and Messiah. Too often we are
content to recognize his anointing as God's Son and to
accept his salvation without submitting to his authority. But
this isn't an option. Either we give him the authority in our
lives or we have an incomplete salvation. The consequence
will be that we will be torn apart by our divided loyalties.

If we hang onto our own authority we miss out on some
of his. In the process we lose out on the ability to deal with
insecurities, fears and anxieties. Remember, it is only as we
give up authority that we will acquire it. After all, his authority is more effective than ours to triumph in every life-
situation. anxiety is often the step-child of compromise.

AUTHORITY AND RESPONSIBILITY

We have already said that responsibility is not viable without appropriate authority. Jesus gives us both responsibility
and the authority adequate for the task. But, by the same
token, when the Lord imparts authority he expects it to be
wielded responsibly.

James and John had to learn this when the Samaritan vil-
lagers insulted their master. They wanted to call down fire
from heaven to destroy these impudent infidels. Jesus
roundly rebuked them and, according to some manuscripts,
said, 'You do not know what kind of spirit you are of, for
the Son of Man did not come to destroy men's lives, but to
save them' (Luke 9:55). This reading is entirely in keeping

with the attitude of Jesus. The Spirit-imparted authority which resided in their own human spirits was not to be used recklessly but in keeping with the master's mission.

At the end of his second letter to the Corinthians Paul warned the church at Corinth that he was coming to visit them again. As a group of Christians they were dear to his heart. Paul had already written to them asking them to sort out some moral issues in their lives. Earlier in this letter he records, 'I wrote to you out of great distress and anguish of heart and with many tears, not to grieve you but to let you know the depth of my love for you' (2 Corinthians 2:4). They had begun to put matters right but more progress was needed. So now Paul writes, 'we cannot do anything against the truth, but only for the truth. We are glad whenever we are weak but you are strong; and our prayer is for your perfection. That is why I write these things when I am absent, that when I come I may not have to be harsh in my use of authority — the authority the Lord gave me for building you up, not for tearing you down' (13:8 – 10).

Paul recognized that he had received apostolic authority from the Lord. This authority was to build the church. Nevertheless, he knew that sometimes it is necessary to demolish before it is possible to build. His authority could serve both purposes. Paul chose to use his authority responsibly by giving the Corinthians the chance to do their own demolition job before he arrived. This would clear the way for him to do what was really in his heart for them, 'I will very gladly spend for you everything I have and expend myself as well,' he says; and, he asks, 'if I love you more, will you love me less?' (12:15).

In an earlier letter to the Corinthians Paul did not stand on his apostolic authority but after pointing out the privations entailed in his apostolic ministry he reminds them: 'Even though you have ten thousand guardians in Christ, you do not have many fathers, for in Christ Jesus I became your father through the gospel' (1 Corinthians 4:15). Elsewhere he speaks just as tenderly to the Christians in Thessalonica. 'As apostles of Christ,' he reports, 'we could have been a burden to you, but we were gentle among you, like a mother caring for her little children. We loved you so much that we were delighted to share with you not only the gospel of God but our lives as well, because you had become so dear to us' (1 Thessalonians 2:7 – 8). Later on he comments, 'you know that we dealt with each of you as a father deals with his own children, encouraging, comforting and urging you to live lives worthy of God' (2:11 – 12).

It seems that whenever Paul had occasion to refer to his undoubted apostolic authority he softened it by speaking of his parental concern for the Christians under his charge. This is because Paul knew that responsible authority grows out of relationships. He founded these churches. This gave him rights, but he preferred to major on his responsibilities.

If Jesus has given us authority, we must use it responsibly. At the same time, if we give him authority in our lives we can surrender the responsibility for the use of that authority to him. This should take the anxiety out of our hearts.

The authority which Jesus gives to us is purely the authority of his life within us. John says: 'to as many as received him he gave the authority to become sons of God' (John 1:12, own translation). We not only became sons through the authority of Jesus but, because we *are* sons, we have *his* authority.

Jesus told his disciples that they could ask anything they wished and it would be given them (John 15:7). There was only one condition: 'If you remain in me and my words remain in you, ask whatever you wish, and it will be given you.' The fruit of the vine comes from living a life which is hidden in that vine. Our responsibility is to stay in him, then we will have authority to act responsibly *for* him.

To be truly in Jesus is to acknowledge his Lordship over every area of a life lived in him. Only then can anxiety be divorced from responsibility. Our responsibilities need never make us anxious because his authority and ours become one.

JESUS, THE AUTHOR OF FAITH OVER ANXIETY

The writer to the Hebrews speaks of Jesus as 'the author and perfector of our faith' (12:2). 'Faith' here does not refer to a static body of doctrine but to the dynamic of belief. Indeed, if we look at this verse in context, the writer is following on from his great portrait gallery of faith in chapter eleven. Developing his theme, he imagines this cluster of Old Testament characters, the 'men of faith', as spectators in the stands watching us running a long-distance race. This race is the life of faith and Jesus is pictured as both the starting marshall and the finishing judge (the author is the initiator, and the perfector is one who completes).

Two things are necessary for us to finish the race. First, to get rid of any entanglements that will hinder our progress and second, to fix our eyes from the start to the finish on Jesus.

> *Our responsibility is to stay in him, then we will have authority to act responsibly* **for** *him.*

Watching the European Championships on television recently, I was impressed with how many officials in the track and field events were themselves former event champions. they make the best judges. Many of the coaches too were former winners, they make the best models.

In the same way, the letter to the Hebrews points out, our starter and finishing judge has run the race before us. From him we can learn some valuable lessons. He scorned the hardship and pain to gain the prize. 'Let us fix our eyes upon Jesus, the author and perfector of our faith, who for the joy that was set before him endured the cross, scorning its shame, and sat down at the right hand of the throne of God.' It cost him a lot to gain the trophy but he refused to be deterred.

When we are going through pain, hardship or discouragement it is easy to lose heart and become anxious, feeling that we will never win through, thinking God has abandoned us. We will not be anxious if we concentrate on our role-model. Isaiah predicted of Jesus and the cross, 'He will see the result of the suffering of his soul and be satisfied' (53:11, Masoretic text).

'Consider him who endured such opposition from sinful men,' exhorts the writer to the Hebrews, 'so that you will not grow weary and lose heart' (12:3). He goes on to say, 'Endure hardship as discipline [because] God is treating you as sons.' Jesus was treated the same way but did not become anxious and did not give up. The authority, and hence the Lordship, of Jesus comes from one who has trod where we tread. 'Let us hold firmly to the faith we profess. For we do not have a high priest who is unable to sympathise with our weaknesses, but we have one who has been tempted in every way, just as we are — yet was without sin' (Hebrews 4:14b, 15).

Jesus initiated our faith, he put the dynamic into us and he will see it through to the end, so why worry? If that faith is compared to a race which requires endurance we should not be surprised that it turns out to be both a marathon and an obstacle race. Nevertheless, the promise is clear, 'he who began a good work in you will carry it on to completion until the day of Jesus Christ' (Philippians 1:6). This means that he is the author of faith over anxiety. He has a moral right to lead us to victory, he has been there before us without succumbing to anxious fear. We can trust the Father, as he did, because the same resources are available to us. Jesus did not walk three feet above the ground — he experienced the same temptations and traumas that we do. He overcame, not because he was divine so that temptation could not touch him, but because, having laid aside the trappings of his divinity, as a perfect man he called upon the resources of his Father through the Holy Spirit. Before he could go about doing good he needed to be anointed by the Holy Spirit at his baptism in the Jordan.

If that faith is compared to a race which requires endurance we should not be surprised that it turns out to be both a marathon and an obstacle race.

Commenting on the assertion of Jesus that, 'whoever believes in me... streams of living water will flow from within him' (John 7:38), John the Evangelist explains: 'Up to that time the Spirit had not been given, since Jesus had not yet been glorified.' This means that Jesus had not yet been enthroned. The Holy Spirit is Christ's coronation gift to the Church. On the Day of Pentecost Peter proclaimed, 'Exalted to the right hand of God, he has received the promised Holy Spirit and has poured out what you now see and hear' (Acts 2:33).

It remains true that the faith-dynamic of the Holy Spirit will not pour out of us until we have *personally* glorified or enthroned Jesus. His Lordship is the key to this dynamic, the antidote to anxiety.

10

Leadership of the Holy Spirit

A nxiety is part of the curse, the result of the Fall. When Adam disobeyed God in the garden of Eden it was because he preferred to follow his wife. As soon as the couple disobeyed God, they became aware of their nakedness and took steps to cover it. Having lost their innocence, they anxiously hid from the Lord among the trees.

Because of disobedience a new note of discord and fear was introduced into their relationship with God. When God called to Adam, 'Where are you?' the man replied, 'I heard you in the garden, and I was afraid because I was naked; so I hid.' The sequence has been repeated time without number, 'I heard...I was afraid...I hid.'

SHIFTING RESPONSIBILITY

The reason Adam gave for his fear was not the true one. He was anxious, not because he was naked, but because he sensed that his nakedness was no longer innocent. The strain was in his relationship with God and with his wife. Disobedience produced an irritability and an accusatory self-righteousness between the couple. When accused Adam said, 'it was the woman you put here with me.' Eve transferred the blame to the serpent. In so doing, both implied that God was somehow at fault in the arrangements he had made!

When we are anxious we often end up blaming God. Whether the accusation is outright or by implication the net result is still the same. 'If only I weren't in this situation,' we complain, 'I would cope better.' Whenever we blame our circumstances for our anxiety or whenever we allow circumstances to create anxiety, we are shifting the responsibility onto God. After all, he is the originator of our circumstances, one way or another.

The real cause of Adam's anxiety lay in his violation of God's command 'You must not eat fruit from the tree that is in the middle of the garden, and you must not touch it, or you will die' (Genesis 3:3). God told the man that the day he disobeyed, he would die. Yet he manifestly lived on for hundreds of years. The sentence cannot therefore have applied only to *physical* death. The day Adam rebelled against God, something within him died. It affected his walk with God; the death was spiritual.

All undue anxiety stems from the fact that man has rebelled against God, has died spiritually and has ceased to trust him. Even when trust is restored and spiritual birth occurs, the seeds of doubt and rebellion, insinuated by Satan, remain. It is these seeds which are the source of our anxiety. To understand this better we need to be aware of the ways in which God chooses to work in our lives.

SPIRIT, SOUL, BODY

There are many passages of Scripture, scattered throughout the Old and New Testaments where the terms 'soul' and 'spirit' are used interchangeably. Nevertheless, there is a difference between the two. The Apostle Paul speaks of this when he says, 'May God himself, the God of peace, sanctify you through and through. May your whole spirit, soul and body be kept blameless at the coming of our Lord Jesus Christ' (1 Thessalonians 5:23). The writer to the Hebrews underlines this analysis when he says, 'The word of God is living and active. Sharper than any double-edged sword, it penetrates even to dividing soul and spirit, joints and marrow; it judges the thoughts and attitudes of the heart' (Hebrews 4:12). Both of these authors distinguish between the soul and the spirit of man. What is the point of the distinction?

When God arrived at the pinnacle of his creation he said, 'Let us make man in our image, in our likeness, and let them rule over the fish of the sea, and the birds of the air, over the livestock, over all the earth, and over all the creatures that move over the ground' (Genesis 1:26). When God proclaimed that he was to make man in his own image, he clearly was not talking about physical likeness, since God is a spiritual entity.

In what, then, lay the similarity? The hidden truth in God's statement is 'let *us* make'. Although one, God is also plural. It takes the rest of Scripture to unfold the reality that God is Father, Son and Holy Spirit. In a parallel manner, man's nature is body, soul and spirit.

Part of the implication of this threefold image of God which is called 'man', is that humans are also intended to make and to rule just as God does. The instant that man, in Adam, disobeyed God, this image was defaced. Man's spirit died within him and his body also began to die. Physical and spiritual death has been within us ever since.

In his natural state, man is at war with God, whether he knows it or not. This is why it takes the God of peace to sanctify us through and through. To sanctify simply means to set aside for God's use. Hence it means 'to be completely his' and, to be completely his, we need to allow him to live in us totally. Only then can we know peace. When we are completely set aside and filled with God himself there can be no anxiety. Anxiety is a lack of trust and results in a fear of his purposes. The remedy, then, is clear but how do we arrive at it?

When the serpent tempted Eve he did so by appealing to her physical senses and to her reason. 'When the woman saw that the fruit of the tree was good for food and pleasing to the eye, and also desirable for gaining wisdom, she took some and ate it' (Genesis 3:6). Her vision and her taste (and presumably her sense of touch and smell) were seduced, while her ears took in the information which ravished her mind. Her disobedience was complete. She came under God's curse and her communion with him was disrupted.

Thus, working through bodily sensations to inform her soul and incite her spirit to rebellion, Satan's victory was complete. Spiritual death came about because the opponent was able to invert God's order. It is God's intention for man's spirit to rule over his soul and for his soul to dominate his body. This is why Paul prays for God to sanctify spirit, soul and body. As our spirit is set aside and filled with God, it will order our thoughts and our actions which stem, in sequence, from our soul and body.

It may help to look at these three aspects of our human composition, in the reverse order.

The Body

There is abundant biblical evidence that we should delight in our physical bodies. The body is part of that Creation from which God stood back, as it were, and pronounced it good. Indeed, 'God saw all that he had made, and it was very good' (Genesis 1:31). The Lord is pleased with his own handiwork of which we, including our bodies, are a part.

True, sin has changed the aspect of what God made and the earth no longer enjoys the pristine quality in which it was created. Nevertheless, the Old Testament, particularly the Psalms, is full of rejoicing at the physical aspects of creation. David says, 'I praise you because I am fearfully and wonderfully made; your works are wonderful, I know that full well' (Psalm 139:14). Even though the same writer complains, 'Surely I was sinful at birth, sinful from the time my mother conceived me' (Psalm 51:5), the balance comes down on the side of rejoicing at the wonder of what God has made.

For too long the church has been trapped in an unbiblical way of thinking about the human body which stems from Greek philosophy. This way of thinking crept into theology after the time of the apostles, particularly through the writing of Augustine. The Greek emphasis was that matter is abhorrent and the flesh is sinful in itself. The body was pictured as a dark, sensual prison and salvation was viewed as the escape of the soul, from a life sentence, into freedom from its jail.

This is profoundly unscriptural. The Bible hope is *Christ in us*; he is our hope of glory precisely because he was raised bodily from the dead. One day, through that same power, we too will receive resurrection bodies and we will become complete — saved, body, soul and spirit. The soul is not what one philosopher has lampooned as 'a ghost in the machine'. It is a vital part of our total makeup and without the body it is meaningless.

King David's awareness of sin expressed in Psalm 51 reminds us that all is not well even with our wonderfully created bodies. Because of sin, the body can be the source of our moral and spiritual downfall. Later, the New Testament letter of Jude speaks of false teachers 'who follow mere natural instincts and do not have the Spirit' (verse 19). Apart from the Holy Spirit, we all tend to follow 'mere natural instincts'. One translation renders this phase as 'sensual'. By this it does not necessarily mean sexually debauched. Rather, it means 'bound by the five senses'.

The fact is that the body is the avenue of our five basic senses: sight, hearing, touch, taste and smell. It is through these channels that we are vitally connected with the outside world. It is not surprising, therefore, that it is through these senses that most of our temptations to sin come. It is our bodily sensations which stimulate the next area of our nature.

The Soul

The biblical view of the soul is complex and there is not scope here to explore it fully. Broadly speaking, when the Bible speaks of 'the soul', the reference is to our ability to think, respond emotionally and to decide. The nearest modern term to what the Bible means by 'the soul' is what we call 'personality'. Apart from our outward physical appearance, it is the soul which constitutes our personhood and denotes our individuality. It is from the soul or personality that we respond at the deepest levels to other persons.

The soul is the source of some of the greatest advances of mankind. It is from the resources of the soul that the human individual subdues the elements, builds cathedrals, sings songs, writes great literature, creates new technology, and dominates other people.

The soul is the fountain of most of what is good and bad about human civilization. It is also true that most religion originates from the soul of man. Much of what passes for worship is simply not spiritual. It is, to borrow a word, 'soulish'. When a person is bound by the senses, every sense-impression is fed into, and dominates, his personality. Thus the soul is controlled by the body. Each thought, emotion and act of the will is dictated by what is received through the senses.

The Apostle Paul has a word for the sense-dominated soul. The Greek word is *sarkikos* which is often translated as 'the flesh'. The NIV, wishing to distinguish between this term and the body, consistently translates Paul's term as 'the sinful nature'. Romans 8 verse 5 reads 'Those who live according to the sinful nature have their minds set on what that nature desires.' The sense-dominated soul, or personality, becomes locked in to what feeds it.

> *It is from the resources of the soul that the human individual subdues the elements, builds cathedrals, sings songs, writes great literature, creates new technology, and dominates other people.*

That is why Paul, elsewhere, urges us to feed our souls on the right sense impressions: 'Finally, brothers, whatever is true, whatever is noble, whatever is pure, whatever is lovely, whatever is admirable — if anything is excellent or praiseworthy — think about such things' (Philippians 4:8). Or, as he puts it in Colossians 3:2, 'Set your minds on things above, not on earthly things.' The soul has the capacity to influence the direction of a man's spirit. The direction it sets will depend on the impulses it receives.

The Spirit

The term 'spirit', when applied to the human spirit, is often used biblically as though it meant the same as 'soul'. It is clear that this is a loose usage of the term because 'soul' and 'spirit' are close in relationship to each other. However, the New Testament also speaks of the spirit in a sense which is obviously unique.

Thus when Jesus was confronted with spiritual obtuseness on the part of religious leaders (Mark 8:12) or with the damaging consequences of sin (John 11:33) he responded in his spirit. When he approached the tomb of his friend Lazarus, Jesus is variously said to be deeply moved or indignant in his spirit, depending on the translation. It was in his spirit (Mark 2:8) that Jesus intuitively knew what men were thinking when they raised objections in their hearts.

What then is the human spirit? Scripture makes it clear that it is the means by which we are aware of God. It is only through our spirit that we are opened up to the spiritual realm.

For instance, Jesus proclaimed in 'the Sermon on the Mount' that it is the poor in spirit who possess the Kingdom of God. We take it that this refers to those who are so aware of their spiritual poverty that they constantly need to call upon God. This is why they realize the Kingship of God over their lives.

Jesus made it clear to Nicodemus, the Jewish spiritual leader who was seeking for truth, that it is only as we are born of the Spirit that we can see the Kingdom. The word often translated 'again' in the phrase 'born again' can also be legitimately translated 'from above'. In spite of the context, this is perhaps a better rendering. Only those who are born from above can see God's Kingdom because it is through the human spirit that God exercises his control over us. As Jesus went on to explain 'Flesh gives birth to flesh, but the Spirit gives birth to spirit' (John 3:6). It is the Holy Spirit who awakens our human spirit so that we are no longer dead in trespasses and sins — that is, spiritually cut off from God.

Speaking of the contrast between the Old and New

Covenants the writer to the Hebrews says in chapter 12, verse 18, 'You have not come to a mountain that can be touched and that is burning with fire...but you have come to Mount Zion, to the heavenly Jerusalem, the city of the living God. You have come to thousands upon thousands of angels in joyful assembly, to the church of the firstborn, whose names are written in heaven. You have come to God, the judge of all men, to the spirits of righteous men made perfect, to Jesus the mediator of a new covenant.'

In other words, the new covenant brings us into a new and spiritual reality. Part of the reality is what historically has been called 'the communion of saints'. That is the spiritual unity of all those throughout the world who are born of the Spirit ('the church of the firstborn'), together with those born-again believers who have already passed on to heaven ('the spirits of religious men made perfect'). For only those who have died in the Lord are made perfect.

Our spirit not only worships and not only grasps spiritual truth, it also reacts to error and detects false teaching.

It is, then, through the Holy Spirit's work in our human spirit that we enter into the spiritual realm. Our spirit is that part of us which is open to God, as we have said. This is why all true worship comes, not primarily from the body or the soul of a person, but from his spirit. That is what Jesus meant when he told the Samaritan woman at the well, 'God is spirit, and his worshippers must worship in spirit and in truth' (John 4:24). So it is that Mary greeted the angelic news that she was going to bear the Saviour of the World with the words 'my spirit rejoices in God my Saviour for he has been mindful of the humble state of his servant' (Luke 1:47). Such worship can only come from the spirit.

All real grasp of truth is through man's spirit. Thus, it is said of Apollos, the Alexandrian convert, in the book of Acts that 'being fervent in spirit he taught accurately' (Acts 18:25, AV). However, there was more that he needed to know, experientially, so Priscilla and Aquila took him in hand and taught him further. If his understanding had been merely intellectual he would never have been taken on deeper in this way.

Our spirit not only worships and not only grasps spiritual truth, it also reacts to error and detects false teaching. In Athens the Apostle Paul's 'spirit was provoked within him as he saw the idols' (Acts 17:16, RSV). The Apostle himself makes it clear in his first Corinthian letter that the Holy Spirit reveals things to us in our spirits which we would never otherwise receive or understand. It is in our spirit that we know the thoughts of God, understand what God has freely given, speak with divine wisdom, and accept the gifts of the Holy Spirit (1 Corinthians 2:8 – 15). Elsewhere he explains that it is the means of being secure in our standing with God, for 'The Spirit himself testifies with our spirit that we are God's children' (Romans 8:16).

A GLORIOUS CHANNEL

If our spirit is such a glorious channel of communication with God it is clear that we must keep that channel open. Through it God intends that we should control both soul and body. The Apostle Paul makes it clear in the eighth chapter of his letter to the Romans that we keep open to God in our spirit as a result of the way we live. 'Those who live according to the sinful nature have their minds set on what that nature desires; but those who live in accordance with the Spirit have their minds set on what the Spirit desires. The mind of sinful man is death, but the mind controlled by the Spirit is life and peace; the sinful mind is hostile to God' (Romans 8:5 – 8).

Paul goes on to comment, 'You, however, are controlled not by the sinful nature but by the Spirit, if the Spirit of God lives in you.' It is arguable that in this equation the first occurrence of the word 'spirit' should be written with a small 's'. The original Greek gives us no clue. If this surmise is correct, what Paul is saying is that if the Holy Spirit lives in us, that is, if he is truly active, then our human spirit is in control of our lives under the direction of the Holy Spirit.

WATERING THE SEED

We began by describing how, since the rebellion of Adam, the seeds of rebellion remain, even in a redeemed life. Preventing these seeds from growing enables us to know the leadership of the Holy Spirit. Paul says, 'if you live according to the sinful nature, you will die; but if by the Spirit you put to death the misdeeds of the body, you will live, because those who are led by the Spirit of God are sons of God' (Romans 8:13 – 14).

The crucified life which we have enables us to walk in step with the Holy Spirit.

In other words, it depends which seed you allow to grow in your life — the seed of Satan or the imperishable seed (see 1 Peter 1:23) by which we are born again. In another passage, in Galatians, chapter 5, Paul lists the manifestations of the sinful nature which include, 'sexual immorality, impurity and debauchery; idolatry and witchcraft; hatred, discord, jealousy, fits of rage, selfish ambition, dissensions, factions and envy; drunkenness and orgies.' These he contrasts with the ninefold fruiting of the Holy Spirit in our lives, namely, 'love, joy, peace, patience, kindness, goodness, faithfulness, gentleness and self-control.'

It all depends upon which seed we water in our lives. The way in which we deal with the seeds of rebellion is by crucifixion. 'Those who belong to Christ Jesus have crucified the sinful nature with its passions and desires,' says Paul in the next verse. There is one step beyond this crucifixion process, 'Since we live by the Spirit,' says Paul — that is, since it is he who gives us spiritual life — 'let us keep in step with the spirit.' The crucified life which we have enables us to walk in step with the Holy Spirit. In keeping with his role as the Counsellor, he leads not from way out in front, but walking alongside us. The word *parakletos*, translated 'Counsellor', literally means 'one called alongside to help'.

Walking step by step with the Holy Spirit is not compatible with anxiety. Moreover, peace is one of the fruits of such a relationship, and peace and anxiety cannot co-exist.

PART
5

WHOLENESS

*Living Without
Anxiety*

11

Indwelling and Outworking

A nxiety is not compatible with the life of God in us. It is through birth from above, the new birth, that we enter the Kingdom of God. Immediately, we are removed from the dark realm of anxiety and the fears which once dominated our lives.

THE SPIRIT AND ANXIETY

The apostle Paul, writing to the Colossians, chapter 1, verse 13, says that God 'has rescued us from the domination of darkness and brought us into the Kingdom of the Son he loves.' Anyone who has suffered from the paralyzing effects of anxiety will know that it is part of the darkness which is Satan's dominion. If we are in the Kingdom of the Son whom God loves, is it conceivable that anxiety can be part of his rule? Clearly, Satan is the sole author of anxiety.

Paul was a realist, he did not preach the modern doctrine 'Come to Christ and your troubles will be over'. Indeed, in the same passage he prayed for the Colossian Christians, 'that you may live a life worthy of the Lord and may please him in every way: bearing fruit in every good work, growing in the knowledge of God, being strengthened with all power according to his glorious might so that you may have great endurance and patience, and joyfully giving thanks to the Father, who has qualified you to share in the inheritance of the saints in the kingdom of light.' The point is, they needed to be strengthened because what lay ahead of them in the Christian life required endurance and patience. You do not need endurance unless you are being heavily tested and you do not need patience unless it involves a lengthy time factor and frequent provocations. Endurance is what takes a marathon runner through the pain to a sense of achievement. Patience is what sustains a mother in bringing a constantly naughty child to maturity.

Paul insists that in such circumstances it is possible joyfully to give thanks to the Father. If we know Christ, it is a statement of fact that we have been transplanted from the realm of darkness into his Son's Kingdom. But Paul realistically points out that God has only *qualified* us to share in *the inheritance* of the saints in the kingdom of light (verse 12). It is possible to live in the sunshine but to insist on keeping one's eyes shut!

The key to taking up the qualification to possess the inheritance of saints in the kingdom of light is simply joyfully to give thanks to Father. Simple, but not easy. It is one thing to quote 'in everything give thanks', it is quite another to do it. Nevertheless a joyful, thankful heart and anxiety cannot co-exist.

It is by the life which God has deposited in us that we learn to rejoice, since that life gives hope. 'Christ in you the hope of glory' (Colossians 1:27), is not merely an ornamental phrase, it is a reality. Paul elsewhere links hope, glory and rejoicing when he says, 'we rejoice in the hope of the glory of God. Not only so, but we also rejoice in our sufferings, because we know that suffering produces perseverance; perseverance, character; and character, hope. And hope does not disappoint us, because God has poured out his love in our hearts by the Holy Spirit, whom he has given us' (Romans 5:2 – 5).

God is in the business of producing character. Because we live in the hope of glory we know how to rejoice in adversity and the end-product is further hope without disappointment. Anxiety arises out of, and causes, disappointment but the Holy Spirit pours out his love into us. He is the ultimate antidote to anxiety.

If we know the Spirit of God has led us into our current situation there can be no cause for anxiety. He works his love in us and, as the Apostle John points out, 'There is no fear in love. But perfect love casts out fear, because fear has to do with punishment. The one who fears it not made perfect in love' (1 John 4:18).

If we are anxious we need to allow the Holy Spirit to mature (perfect) us in love to the point where fear and anxiety are driven out.

THE SPIRIT AND ADOPTION

Paul describes the Holy Spirit as 'the Spirit of adoption', and, he adds, 'by him we cry *Abba*, Father' (Romans 8:15). It is through him that we receive our adoption as sons.

This is not a sexist statement. The term 'sons', here, applies to Christians of both sexes. The New Testament uses the term 'son' in relation to adoption simply because in those times it was normally the son of the family who inherited from the father. This is why, speaking of Christians, Paul insists, 'You are *all* sons of God through faith in Christ Jesus, for all of you who were baptised into Christ have clothed yourself with Christ.' We are all treated as sons — that is, heirs — whether male or female, because we are clothed in the regalia of God's unique Son, Jesus. More than that, from God's standpoint, we are actually in his Son. From the angle of our inheritance the Father treats us as though *we* were his only Son.

Paul's insistence that all Christians, whatever their gender, are sons is followed by his famous impassioned statement in Galatians 3:28: 'There is neither Jew nor Greek, slave nor free, male nor female, for you are all one in Christ Jesus.' And, he reminds us, 'if you belong to Christ you are all Abraham's seed, and heirs according to the promise' (verse 29). Our inheritance comes by faith, not by gender.

All this may sound strange to modern ears. That is because our customs of adoption are different from those of New Testament days. To us, adoption is legally giving family rights to someone who is not naturally a member of the family, as in the case of an orphan. This means that an adopted person may not share the family likeness, but he is legally co-opted as a member of the family with equal rights.

Our inheritance comes by faith, not by gender.

Everyone who enters God's family does so by spiritual birth, as Jesus made clear to Nicodemus. Every member of the family is conceived through God's Word, born of the Spirit and shares the Father's likeness. This is why the Apostle Peter says, 'he has given us his very great and precious promises, so that through them you may participate in the divine nature' (2 Peter 1:4). To use a different figure of speech employed by Jesus, nobody will get into the wedding feast without the provided wedding garment.

Adoption, to Paul, meant something different. In wealthy households the son who was the heir to the family fortune was cared for by an appointed tutor. This mentor's job was to bring the child to maturity, fitting him to take up his inheritance and wield power for himself. 'What I am saying,' Paul comments, 'is that as long as the heir is a child, he is no different from a slave, although he owns the whole estate. He is subject to guardians and trustees until the time set by his father' (Galatians 4:1 – 2).

Adoption, then, was the legal means by which the child who was already a natural member of the family came formally into the title of the estate. At adoption he became responsible for his own destiny with the full financial, social and legal resources of his inheritance in his possession. Spiritually, we are born into the family of God by the action of the Holy Spirit. By the intervention of the same Spirit we are adopted and we come into our full inheritance as sons.

Freedom from anxiety is a blood-bought right of every child of God.

Many Christians do not know this; or, if they know it, they do not practise it. It is as though adoption has been proclaimed and the inheritance conferred upon them in their absence. How can we receive the privileges of adoption and continue to be weighed down by anxiety? The resources of our Father's estate are more than adequate to meet our needs and they are ours to use. Because of our adoption we can command circumstances rather than cower before them.

Paul says that before our birth and adoption into the family of God we were treated like slaves by the world. 'When we were children, we were in slavery under the basic principles of the world,' he comments. This phrase can be rendered, 'we were in slavery under the elemental spirits of the world'. In other words, we were controlled by forces beyond ourselves.

This *was* certainly cause for anxiety but such is no longer the case. The more we live as though it were still the case, the more we will be practically enslaved although legally, and actually, free.

Freedom from these principles, or spirits, is part of the work of Christ on the cross where he took on principalities and powers and openly defeated them. Hence freedom from anxiety is a blood-bought right of every child of God for,

> when the time had fully come, God sent his Son, born of a woman, born under law, to redeem those under law, *that we might receive the full rights of sons* [our italics]. Because you are sons, God sent the Spirit of his Son into our hearts, the Spirit who calls out '*Abba*, Father'. So you are no longer a slave, but a son; and since you are a son, God has also made you an heir.
>
> *Galatians 4:4 – 7*

Adoption means freedom because we not only share his nature, we also share his inheritance — that is, authority given by the Holy Spirit to banish anxiety.

THE SPIRIT AND ACCEPTANCE

If we are adopted by God as his sons, it follows that we are accepted by him. Modern translations of Ephesians 1, verse 6 speak of the grace which God has freely given us. It was a true spiritual instinct which led the King James Version translators to express this differently. 'He made us accepted in the Beloved,' their version runs.

God *has* accepted us through the activity of the Holy Spirit in our lives. As Peter explained to Cornelius, the Roman centurion in Acts chapter 10, 'I now realise how true it is that God does not show favouritism, but accepts men from every nation who fear him and do what is right' (Acts 10:35). This acceptance of a Gentile seeker was ratified when the gift of the Holy Spirit was poured upon him with accompanying signs. What God did for Cornelius, he is prepared to do for all who truly seek him.

Once the Lord takes us in hand we are *permanently* accepted by him. Jesus said, 'whoever comes to me I will never drive away' (John 6:37). Jesus' relationship with us is solid and unwavering. When he accepts us, he commits himself to us so that, provided we continue to the end, we are safe. 'My sheep listen to my voice,' he says, 'I know them and they follow me. I give them eternal life and they shall never perish; no-one can snatch them out of my hand. My Father who, has given them to me, is greater than all; no-one can snatch them out of my Father's hand.' And, lest we should be tempted to think there might be any fumbling between the Father and the Son, he adds: 'I and the Father are one' (John 10:27 – 29).

In this acceptance that we enjoy from God there is a security which should enable us to lay anxiety aside. It is good to know that whatever we may fear, or whatever we may feel, God sees us as his children. Because he has given birth to us and has given us the adoption rights as sons, he will never fail us or reject us. In fact he seals his acceptance with love-gifts which go beyond those showered upon their children by earthly fathers. These gifts are ours for the asking. As Jesus himself pointed out, 'If you then, though you are evil, know how to give good gifts to your children, how much more will your Father in heaven give the Holy Spirit to those who ask him!' (Luke 11:13).

In accepting us, and sealing his acceptance, God also accepts our prayers. John's measure of certainty is simple: 'This is the confidence we have in approaching God: that if we ask anything according to his will, he hears us. And if we know that he hears us — whatever we ask — we know that we have what we asked of him' (1 John 5:14 – 15).

Of course, this might give rise to further anxiety. How can I know that I am asking according to God's will? There are two ways of testing this. Jesus taught that if we remain in him, so bearing fruit, 'then the Father will give you whatever you ask in my name' (John 15:16). Remaining in him is not difficult, it is just a matter of doing what he tells us to do and staying in his love. Secondly, when we are not sure what his will is, the Holy Spirit within us leaps to our rescue, 'the Spirit helps us in our weakness. We do not know what we ought to pray,' admits Paul, 'but the Spirit himself intercedes for us with groans that words cannot express. And he who searches our hearts knows the mind of the Spirit, because the Spirit intercedes with the saints in accordance with God's will' (Romans 8:26 – 27).

At every level the Holy Spirit secures our acceptance with the Father. It is up to us to recognize this and relax in the fact. The fact is indisputable; our enjoyment of it is more problematic. As we have discussed in the previous chapter, we can see from Romans chapter 8 that it all depends on our mind-set or mental attitude. If our mind is set on the old, carnal nature we will not enjoy our acceptance by Christ and by his Father.

However, if our minds are fixed on spiritual reality we can be overcomers.

> **In all these things we are more than conquerors, through him who loved us. For I am convinced that neither death nor life, neither angels nor demons, neither the present or the future, nor any powers, neither height nor depth, nor anything else in all creation, will be able to separate us from the love of God that is in Christ Jesus our Lord.'**   *Romans 8:37 – 39*

In other words, nothing that makes us anxious can separate us from God's love. It follows, then, that neither can anxiety itself.

THE HOLY SPIRIT AND CHARACTER

At the end of chapter 10 we spoke of the fruits of the Holy
Spirit in contrast with the seeds of rebellion sown in the
human heart as a consequence of the fall of Adam (see
Galatians chapter 5). Now it is time to push that idea a little
further.

A great deal is currently being written and taught about
the gifts of the Holy Spirit. These are essential equipment for
getting the job done which God requires from his church.
Unfortunately, the whole issue of gifts tends to be divisive.
People either rationalize them into a mere heightening of
natural human qualities or they elevate them to a position of
importance which they were never meant to assume.

Spiritual gifts are of the utmost importance as a resource
for getting God's work done. For too long they have been
neglected. Jesus told the first disciples, 'you will receive
power when the Holy Spirit comes upon you; and you will
be my witnesses' (Acts 1:8). The gifts of the Holy Spirit are
part of that power-pack which was first evidenced at
Pentecost.

Nevertheless, God has an even more important objective.
He is concerned to impart character as we co-operate with
the Holy Spirit in progressing to maturity. This is a much
slower process. Mention of the fruit of the Holy Spirit
implies growth and growth takes time. The gifts of the Holy
Spirit are given in an instant without regard to character.
True, we may have to develop in the wise use of these gifts
but this is where character comes in. Some of the greatest
tragedies in the lives of Christians have occurred where gift-
ing far outstrips character. For those of us willing to press on
in the exercise of spiritual gifts there will always be a distance between our character and the gifts we receive from
the Holy Spirit. It is when the gap becomes too great that
disaster looms.

This may be why, when Paul lists the qualities required of an elder, only one refers to a spiritual gift — he must be 'able to teach'. The rest have to do with character. Here is the score:

> the overseer must be above reproach, the husband of but one wife, temperate, self-controlled, respectable, hospitable, able to teach, not given to drunkenness, not violent but gentle, not quarrelsome, not a lover of money. He must manage his own family well and see that his children obey him with proper respect. (If anyone does not know how to manage his own family, how can he take care of God's church?) He must not be a recent convert, or he may become conceited and fall under the same judgement as the devil. He must also have a good reputation with outsiders, so that he will not fall into disgrace.   *1 Timothy 3:2 – 7*

At least three of these qualities coincide with the fruit of the Spirit listed in Galatians, chapter five. God is concerned more with character in church leaders than he is with gifts, precisely because he is seeking to produce maturity of character in every member of the church. Characterless leaders will not produce character in the family of God.

Where does this character come from? Surely it is from allowing the Holy Spirit to be constantly at work in our lives to change our attitudes, getting rid of the bad and fostering the good.

When Jesus wanted to illustrate our relationship with him, he said that he is the vine and we are the branches. This does not mean that Jesus is the stock or trunk while we are added on to become his branches. Jesus said, 'I am the vine.' The vine is everything: roots, trunk, branches, tendrils, leaves and fruit. We are in him as part of the whole. It is his life flowing through us — the sap of the Holy Spirit — that produces the fruit of character.

Actually, the fruit of the Holy Spirit is a transcript of the character of Jesus. Some commentators suggest that rather than a cluster of fruit, like grapes on a vine, the fruit *is* love, and the other eight qualities are components of that love. On this understanding love comprises: 'joy, peace, patience, gentleness, goodness, faithfulness, meekness and self-control.'

This may be so. Certainly in his great passage on love in 1 Corinthians 13, Paul demonstrates the love of Christ in action. This passage is the nearest thing we have in the New Testament to a portrait of Jesus. Try rendering the passage with the name of Jesus substituted for the word 'love'. It then becomes:

> Jesus is patient, Jesus is kind. He does not envy, he does not boast, he is not proud, he is not rude, he is not self-seeking, he is not easily angered, he keeps no record of wrongs. Jesus does not delight in evil but always rejoices with the truth. He always protects, always trusts, always hopes, always perseveres. Jesus never fails.

It fits! What a perfect picture of Jesus! Now try substituting your own name for the word 'love'. The difference between the two readings is the degree of character which the Holy Spirit needs to work in you.

The list is not exclusive. The Holy Spirit does not impart these characteristics to us as passive subjects either. We have our part to play.

The Apostle Peter has a character-list which effectively underscores this point (my italics):

> *Make every effort* to add to your faith goodness; *and* to goodness, knowledge; *and* to knowledge, self-control; *and* to self-control, perseverance; *and* to perseverance, godliness; *and* to godliness, brotherly kindness; *and* to brotherly kindness, love. For if you possess these qualities in increasing measure, they will keep you from

> being ineffective and unproductive in your knowledge
> of our Lord Jesus Christ.   *2 Peter 1:5 – 8*

You may protest, 'I thought we weren't supposed to add anything to faith?' It is true, faith is foundational, but it is only by faith that we can add to faith. Yet, in context, it appears that these qualities grow out of participating in the divine nature. Two things are clear. First, development of character requires effort; second, these qualities come by addition (something different in kind or quality) and by increase (something greater in quantity). There is always room in our character development for more growth. The more our character qualities blossom, the less room there will be for the blight of anxiety.

BE ANXIOUS FOR NOTHING

In the fourth chapter of his letter to the Philippians, the Apostle Paul makes what appears to be an impossible demand. 'Do not be anxious about anything,' he instructs.

Anxiety seems to be a natural reaction to our circumstances which is impossible to avoid. This is just what is wrong with anxiety — it is a purely *natural* reaction. It is the overt response of the natural man, not of our true spiritual nature. We have seen that it is this spiritual nature which God is seeking to grow in us through his Holy Spirit.

Paul was no armchair theoretician in this matter of overcoming anxiety. Indeed, at the time he wrote this injunction to the Christians in Philippi he was himself languishing in a Roman jail. At the beginning of the letter it is clear that at least one group of Christians had it in for Paul. They were engaging in evangelistic activity in such a way as to make Paul's situation in prison more difficult. Surely this was a cause for frustration and anxiety? But, no, Paul exclaims: 'what does it matter? The important thing is that in every way, whether from false motives or true, Christ is preached. And because of this I rejoice' (Philippians 1:18).

Nothing banishes the sense of the presence of the Lord quicker than anxiety.

Paul had learned to deal with the centre of self. The proclamation of the gospel was more important than petty personal considerations; even when those considerations involved personal discomfort and pain. He knew that at the core of anxiety is an undue self-regard. Because he had learned to deal with this Paul could genuinely say, 'Do not be anxious about anything'. He had tested it and had come up with the answer — just turn everything over to God and leave it with him.

Peace is the opposite of anxiety and Paul had learned that entrusting matters to God brings a deep peace to the human heart. Thus he says, 'in everything, by prayer and petition with thanksgiving, present your requests to God. And the peace of God which transcends all understanding, will guard your hearts and minds in Christ Jesus.' What a privilege it is to know heart and mind being guarded by the unruffled peace of God. The source of this tranquility, the certainty that God will deal with our requests lies in Paul's preceding statement: 'The Lord is near. Do not be anxious for anything.' Nothing banishes the sense of the presence of the Lord quicker than anxiety. Nothing obliterates anxiety sooner than his nearness.

REJOICE, REJOICE!

In fact Paul advocates not only the calm of the peace of God in our hearts and minds. Before that he had told the

Philippians, 'Rejoice in the Lord always'. And in case that sounded too hard, 'I will say it again: Rejoice!' (4:4).

Such rejoicing in adverse circumstances is not natural. Nor is it 'unnatural', rather it is spiritual. That is to say, it comes from the work of the Holy Spirit in our lives.

There's a spiritual song which underlines this truth:

> **Rejoice, rejoice Christ is in you,**
> **The hope of glory in your hearts,**
> **He lives! He lives! His breath is in you**
> **Arise, a mighty army, we arise.**

We will only rise under the blows of circumstance if we can positively rejoice in it.

Again, this was no armchair opinion held by Paul. He told the Philippians, 'I rejoice greatly in the Lord that you have renewed your concern for me' (4:10). Apparently, the Philippian Church had sent Paul a gift to sustain him in prison. Typically, Paul's rejoicing was not because of the creature comforts gained by this gift, much as he enjoyed them. 'I am not saying this because I am in need,' he records, 'for I have learned to be content whatever the circumstances.'

Paul was grateful for the gift in itself but he rejoiced more in the fact that it was a sign of the spiritual growth and maturity of the Philippian Church. 'Not that I am looking for a gift, but I am looking for what may be credited to your account. I have received full payment and even more' (4:17). In this way he was able to turn the gift into an occasion, from prison, to encourage those who were physically free. He did this by turning a personal gesture on their part into an act of worship. 'I am amply supplied, now that I have received from Epaphroditus the gifts you sent. They are a fragrant offering, an acceptable sacrifice, pleasing to God' (4:18).

Paul was able to experience peace in prison because he

turned all of his anxieties over to God. He was able to rejoice because, instead of feeling sorry for himself in his situation, he was able to see God working in his life and the lives of others, even in difficult situations.

LEARNING THE SECRET

In this way the apostle learned to live above circumstances and the anxieties which they can create. 'I have learned the secret of being content in any and every situation, whether well fed or hungry, whether living in plenty or in want,' he says in verse 12 of chapter 4.

We too need to learn the secret of contentment which banishes anxiety. The peace of God is not an undisturbed calm but a deep-rooted conviction of the goodness of the purposes which come from his throne. The secret of being content is staying close to the purposes of God and resting secure in the power which he gives to contend with circumstances.

Let Paul have the last word: 'I can do everything through him who gives me strength.'

12

Living in the Word

There is a mountain about four miles away from our house. Sometimes, when I (Dick) want to get away from everything, I drive to the foot of the mountain and then walk up it, branching either towards moorland or forest, depending which part of the ridge I choose.

The first part of the climb takes me up a steep lane and through a farmyard before coming out onto the open mountainside. Frequently, the first part of the climb is uncomfortable. This is especially true during the summer when my head is surrounded by buzzing flies and biting midges. To the casual onlooker I must look like a mad frustrated conductor as I wave my arms to keep the insects at bay!

It is during this first part of the climb that I get my wind and my legs ache before settling into a steady walking rhythm. Once out onto the open mountain, surrounded by nothing but sheep and clear views, the flies drop away in the cool breeze. The annoyances are left behind until at the summit I can see around me for miles.

Looking down upon the town and the uncluttered countryside beyond I usually get a different perspective on life. Troubles, too, seem to fall away in the mountain air and it becomes much easier to spend time with the Lord. Somehow insects are not the only distraction which is left behind as I listen to what he has to say.

SPENDING TIME IN THE UPLANDS

God's Word, the Bible, reminds me of those mountain walks. Annoyances and distractions can so easily put a person off from tackling the ascent. All the same, the effort is worth it. Getting familiar with Scripture and obeying its teaching is as spiritually bracing as a mountain walk.

It takes effort to live in God's word but the only way to overcome anxiety is tied to the Bible. We need to spend time in the uplands of biblical truth. God's will is to be found in his word. Indeed his word *is* his will for us. Constant exercise in it will refresh the spirit, cleansing us and making way for the indwelling of God of which we have already spoken.

When anxiety grips the soul, it takes the fresh vistas and renewed perspective of Scripture to bring us to our senses.

EFFORT IS REQUIRED

Like the mountain climb, effort is required to live in God's word. It does not come naturally or easily.

The Psalmist was aware of this; in Psalm 119, verse 9 he asks, 'How can a young man keep his way pure?' And he provides the answer, 'By living according to your word' (NIV). However, the answer is not as easy to work out as it sounds. Note the active verbs which the psalmist outlines in the next seven verses which make up that stanza of the psalm:

v. 10 — I *seek* you with all my heart
v. 11 — I have *hidden* your word in my heart

v. 13　—　With my lips I *recount* all the laws that
　　　　　come from your mouth
v. 14　—　I *rejoice* in *following* your statutes
v. 15a　—　I *meditate* on your precepts
v. 15b　—　I *consider* your ways
v. 16a　—　I *delight* in your decrees
v. 16b　—　I *will not neglect* your word

These nine directives indicate the considerable effort required to live in God's word. In contrast, the Psalmist only asks two things from God in return: 'Do not let me stray from your commands' (verse 10) and 'teach me your decrees' (verse 12). The truth is that God has provided the spiritual food and support we need in Scripture. He will not assimilate it for us, we have to feed on what he has provided.

LIVE BIBLICALLY

Some time ago, with a member of our team, I ministered to a young woman who was suffering from hypoglycaemia. This is a potentially dangerous condition which requires a careful watch on the diet, particularly on levels of sugar intake. She was a very active and committed Christian worker in a full-time evangelistic team which worked through drama. As we talked, she was asked if she could date the onset of her condition. It soon became obvious that this was not her only or most severe problem.

The disease began after the final separation of her parents who were Mormons. For eleven years she was shuttled between the homes of her father and mother to live, as it suited them. Little thought appears to have been taken for the emotional needs of their daughter. In the process she became unstable and insecure until she found Christ as her Saviour. Nevertheless, her illness continued.

As we prayed into the area of these inner hurts and brought healing of the emotions, she found complete release for the first time. She also found a security in Christ which meant she no longer needed to strive to please the Lord through Christian service.

Afterwards we sat down to tea. It was only after Val had consumed an enormous helping of dessert and ice-cream that we realized God had also healed her of her physical condition! We encouraged her to leave the roving life of an itinerant evangelist and settle down with a stable Christian family for a time. In this way we felt she could live out some of the biblical principles she had learned. And so it turned out.

That same afternoon another young woman was visiting our home. She too was troubled but she had been counselled and prayed with frequently with scant success. On seeing Val's deliverance and healing Sue said, 'but I need deliverance too.' It was the heart-cry of a self-centred little girl within the heart of the grown-up woman.

One of the team turned to her, not unkindly and said gently, 'Sue, you have been counselled more times than I have had hot dinners. What you need now is to get up and to begin to live biblically!'

This may sound harsh but it was excellent advice. Many of us expect an instant answer to problems when the answer already lies in God's word. Praying in power over a person will only achieve temporary answers unless their will is surrendered to be obedient to the Bible.

EXPECTATIONS OF KINGS

In the Old Testament even kings were expected to live according to the standard of God's Law. Indeed, the historical books of Kings and Chronicles measured the success of a monarch's reign not by his political success or military achievements but by the extent to which he measured up to God's standards.

Long before Israel appointed its first king, God foresaw it would happen even though it wasn't his best desire for the nation. Anticipating that time, God instructed Moses to tell the people, 'When you enter the land the Lord your God is giving you and have taken possession of it and settled in it, and you say, "Let us set a King over us like all the nations around us," be sure to appoint over you the King the Lord your God chooses' (Deuteronomy 17:14 – 15).

What better way can there be to know the direction we should take but to 'follow carefully all the words of this law?'

In order to provide guidelines as to the sort of man God would accept as king they were told he was to be a man 'from among your own brothers'. He must not be acquisitive in the area of horses (military power), wives (sexual power) or of silver and gold (financial power). Rather, when a king was appointed he was to become a man of the word of God. He was to be left in no doubt as to what this would mean: 'When he takes the throne of his Kingdom, he is to write for himself on a scroll a copy of this law, taken from that of the priests, who are Levites. It is to be with him, and he is to read it all the days of his life so that he may learn to revere the Lord his God and follow carefully all the words of this law and these decrees and not consider himself better than his brothers and turn from the law to the right or to the left. Then he and his descendants will reign a long time over his kingdom in Israel' (Deuteronomy 17:18 – 20).

This was excellent advice to a king on how to rule successfully. We, too, are called to rule over our own lives. What better way can there be to know the direction we should take but to 'follow carefully all the words of this law?' Of course, we are now under the 'new covenant' and we need to know how the old covenant law applies to us in terms of principles rather than the letter. Nevertheless, if we immerse ourselves in God's law as God intended his Kings to do, we will rule our lives better.

It is worth noticing the way in which these kings were intended to relate to God's word. First, they had to copy it out by hand from a correct version. The Law in those days only amounted to the five books of Moses. Still, it was a daunting task to copy it out by hand. It isn't clear how many, or if any, of the subsequent kings of Israel obeyed this injunction. Yet God's intentions are clear: it was so that they would be fully familiar with the Law and own it for themselves. Knowing Scripture is one thing — it is evident even the Devil does this — ownership of its teaching is entirely another. If we took on board the teaching of God's word, we would be much freer from the ravages of anxiety.

Second, 'it is to be with him'. The King was to carry the law around. It was to be a constant resource. Moreover, he was to read it daily ('all the days of his life') not as a barren exercise, but in order to obey it. The results of daily reading were meant to be twofold: 'That he may learn to revere the Lord his God' and '[that he may] follow carefully all the words of this law and these decrees'. Daily reading was to lead to daily worship and daily obedience. Reverence for God and practice of his basic principles for life are sound prescriptions for living free from anxiety.

THE CULT OF CONFESSION

There is a current teaching regarding positive confession. According to it, if we constantly speak positive things, we will receive the things which we speak out. There is a lot of common sense in the view that if we speak positively this will lead to positive attitudes which will in turn produce positive behaviour. This is a truism, but it is not born from the Bible. Much less is the view that speaking out positive confessions will secure for us what we are speaking out. For instance, I might want a new car of a particular make, model and colour. In praying to receive what I want, it is good to be specific with God. After all, it is much more difficult for him to answer vague generalities. Nevertheless, speaking out, or confessing, what I want will not necessarily bring it. God may see that I do not need it or that to receive that particular answer might be bad for my character.

In our work, we have seen people 'confessing' all sorts of things which God never intended for them. Failure to receive has often given rise to a sense of guilt or, worse, to cynicism about God's willingness to answer. Dealing with anxiety by speaking out the imagined answers to our needs can make matters worse. The cult of confession can heighten anxiety because that which has been confessed has not been received.

> *Failure to receive has often given rise to a sense of guilt or, worse, to cynicism about God's willingness to answer.*

There is, however, more than a grain of truth in this teaching. Taken in the wrong direction it is at best profoundly unbiblical, at worst, damaging. But the fact is that Scripture has many positive statements to make about us and our relationship with God. It is good to look up these statements and begin to speak them out loud to ourselves. They will confirm God's good purposes towards us.

Before we speak out the positives of God's word it is good to take them thoroughly into our hearts and minds. The Psalmist says 'with my lips I will recount all the laws that come from your mouth' (Psalm 119:13), but he does not do so until he claims 'I have hidden your word in my heart that I might not sin against you' (Psalm 119:11).

SOME PRACTICAL STEPS

How can we take in God's word so that we can begin to confess it and live it out? We have already seen some of the practical steps that can be taken to live biblically: first, read God's word daily; second, turn what you read into worship; third, meditate upon what you have read; fourth, memorize God's word; fifth, study it in depth and sixth, begin to put God's word into practice by obeying it. In closing we will comment briefly on each of these steps.

1. Daily Reading

If we are to become familiar with God's word, we need to read it regularly. In the past, many of us have felt trapped by the chore of the daily 'Quiet Time'. Reading the Bible should not be a chore but a delight. It becomes a chore when we hurriedly fit it into the day like some fetish which must be consulted.

It still remains true that the best way to be regular about reading Scripture is to do it every day. Not that we feel condemned when some emergency occurs to prevent it. Gone should be the days when we fear the day's events because we haven't read the Bible. We must not treat God's word as some kind of talisman. Otherwise we will become like the

Pharisees who wore Scripture texts tied round their arms or even on their foreheads!

Daily reading becomes more meaningful if we base it on some plan. Several Bible reading programmes with printed notes are available. They are usually graded according to reading ability or spiritual experience. Even better, use some of the popular handbooks or commentaries to discover some of the background for yourself. As you read, ask God what he wants to say to you from it.

2. Worshipping through the word

We have seen that the Old Testament kings were meant to read the law so that they would revere God. Revere means 'to hold in awe' and hence 'to worship'. The Bible becomes much more meaningful when we use it to worship the Lord.

Scripture teaches so many fresh things about the nature of God, his ways, his intentions for us and his plan for the world. Quarry out some of these facts from your daily reading and turn them into reasons to worship him.

As you read about the creation, tell God how blessed you are by what he has made. Praise him for his creative ability and remind yourself that this same ability is turned towards your circumstances. Look up the names of God, find out what they reveal about his character and thank him for those aspects of his nature. Tell yourself that they apply to you as his child. Begin to turn the words of Scripture into song and use them to worship God.

These are only a few of the ways in which you can worship God through reading the Bible. Worship dispels anxiety. What do you think Paul and Silas felt like in the Philippian jail? As they sang and worshipped God, their circumstances changed. We don't know whether they used Scripture to worship in the direct way we have described.

The truth is, all true worship is based on Scripture anyway. It is the only true source of anything we know about God.

3. Meditate on what you read

There are several Bible passages which encourage us to meditate on God's word. Contemplation and meditation are foreign to modern western life. That is why we tend to associate meditation with mystical eastern religions. Meditation in that form is dangerous. Biblical meditation is different and it's not at all mysterious.

Meditation in the biblical sense is simply to take a passage and turn it over in the mind until you have extracted every ounce of meaning from it. Successful meditation is analagous to an animal chewing the cud. Have you ever seen a sheep not chewing? Usually a sheep is either grazing or it will be gazing into the middle distance chewing what has already been swallowed and regurgitated.

For the bulk of the day, the sheep near our home tear away at the grass as if it is going out of fashion! When they are not doing that they bring up what they have eaten in order to chew it more thoroughly. Just so, you can take a sentence of Scripture turning it around in your mind, thinking through what it means and letting it speak to you. Ask yourself simple questions about the passage: what does it mean? who is it about? does it include me? what can I learn about God's dealings? and so on. Once mentally chewed over like this, a text is difficult to forget. This brings us to the next step.

4. Memorize Scripture

Meditation is an excellent first step towards memorizing Scripture. But, why memorize Bible passages? The answer is simple, you never know when you might need them!

In Bible times Jewish boys memorized whole books of

the Old Testament. Jesus clearly was no exception. This is evident from the passages he quotes or alludes to in the course of his teaching. Perhaps his most effective use of this knowledge was when Satan tempted him in the wilderness, even misquoting Scripture to do so. In each case Jesus replied 'it is written'.

One of the most efficient means to combat anxiety is to memorize scriptures which deal with the issue. Are you afraid of men's opinions? Anxious about your reputation? There are many passages beginning with the command 'fear not' which are useful for anxious people to memorize. Why not learn them? Similarly, for almost every anxiety there is a Scripture, which, when memorized and recalled, will remind you of God's answer.

5. Study the word

Not everyone is equally equipped to study God's word. All the same, almost all of us can push it a little further than merely reading it. Some basic background reading, or the use of a concordance can help tease out the meaning of a passage. Using a Bible handbook or encyclopedia can help us know a little about the customs and daily life of the times in which a Bible passage is set, and so bring it to life.

More systematic Bible study can be achieved through correspondence courses or through a Bible study group in your local church. It should be said that all study of the Bible is with a view to applying the truths learned in daily life.

6. Applying the word

This brings us to the final discipline of the word of God: obeying it. All of the other approaches to Scripture which we have outlined are aimed at applying it in life. The only reason for getting to know the Bible better is that we might put it into practice.

Paul wrote to the young Timothy encouraging him in his ministry. A study of Paul's letters reveals that Timothy was young, felt underpowered and inexperienced, was timid and did not enjoy very good health. What a prescription for anxiety in a young missionary charged with apostolic responsibility!

It is only by living in the word of God that we can cast off the shackles of anxiety and be free to perform the functions for which God intends us.

Paul reminds him that he has two resources. These are the power and gifts of the Holy Spirit, 'I remind you to fan into flame the gift of God, which is in you through the laying on of my hands. For God did not give us a spirit of timidity, but a spirit of power, of love and of self-discipline' (2 Timothy 1:6 – 7). His second resource was Scripture, 'as for you, continue in what you have learned and have become convinced of, because you know those from whom you learned it, and how from infancy you have known the holy Scriptures, which are able to make you wise for salvation through faith in Christ Jesus. All Scripture is God-breathed and is useful for teaching, rebuking, correcting and training in righteousness, so that the man of God may be thoroughly equipped for every good work' (2 Timothy 3:14 – 17).

Clearly, Timothy could only be equipped through paying attention to Scripture. The word 'equipped', which is used elsewhere of mending nets, means 'to render adequate for its intended purpose'.

It is only by living in the word of God that we can cast off the shackles of anxiety and be free to perform the functions for which God intends us.

Appendix

Stress & Anxiety — What's the difference?

Stress and anxiety are not the same thing. This is evident because different people cope with the same stress stimuli in different ways. One person may cope with these 'stressors' by heightened performance, they are merely stimulated into peak action. Another person, or even the same person at another time, may respond to the same 'stressors' by a failure to cope and accompanying feelings of anxiety and unease. However, as we have seen, chronic or misplaced anxiety is due to more than just stress. It has its roots in mental and spiritual conditions and we can also take practical steps to do something about these. It is possible to be anxious yet not be in a state of stress. The converse is also true.

In his helpful booklet on *Breaking Free From Stress* Bob Dix comments on the symptoms of extreme stress. He says that the brain:

> Receives stress signals
> Its frequency increases from 8-12 to 13-21 cycles per second
> This produces feelings of fear or anxiety
> The brain loses the ability to concentrate
> It prepares the body for action
> It releases 30 hormones into the bloodstream

He points out that the body reacts in the following ways:

> Pupils dilate
> Mouth is dry
> Muscles tense ready for action
> Breathing is faster
> Heart beats faster, blood pressure rises
> Digestion slows down or stops
> The stomach prepares to empty itself by a feeling of wanting to vomit or defecate
> Sweating begins

Warning bells signalling the onset of anxiety

Some Affects On The Mind	Some Affects On The Body
Anger rises	Body shakes/tremors/ heart palpitations
Patience wears thin	
Tension headaches	Muscle tightening
Tiredness	Paralysis of movement
Negative thoughts	Loss or gain in appetite
Sense of panic	Indigestion
Confusion	Fatigue
Fear	Nervous feeling
Self-pity	Exhaustion
State of limbo	Sleeplessness
Vengeance	Strain
State of shock	Diminishing health
Sense of guilt	Over or underweight
Depressed	Ulcers
Sense of insecurity	Lack of motivation
Sense of hopelessness	Quick/slow speech

These symptoms may not be serious when we experience them in short bursts but if they become constant then we are heading for trouble.

Selective Bible verses for combating anxiety

Psalm 11; 16; 23; 27:1-6; 37:1-9; 46; 62:1-7; 91; 139; Matthew 5:13,14; John 1:12; 14:1-4; 15:1-17; Acts 1:8; Romans 5:1; 8:1,28,33,35; 1 Corinthians 3:16; 6:17,20; 12:27; 2 Corinthians 5:17,18,21, 6:1; Galatians 5:16-25; Ephesians 1:1,5,13,14, 2:6,10,18,19, 3:12; 6:10-18; Philippians 1:6, 2:6, 3:20; 4:4-9; 4:13; Colossians 1:13,14; 1 Thessalonians 5:22-24; 2 Timothy 1:7; Hebrews 4:16; 1 John 5:1

Personal Checklist

Path to Anxiety

	Sometimes	Often	Always
I am aggressive	☐	☐	☐
I don't feel blessed	☐	☐	☐
I feel constantly in need	☐	☐	☐
I am often in turmoil	☐	☐	☐
I feel blocked	☐	☐	☐
I feel humiliated	☐	☐	☐
I don't make a difference	☐	☐	☐
I never enjoy much	☐	☐	☐
I don't laugh as much	☐	☐	☐
I am not interested	☐	☐	☐
I am mostly disappointed	☐	☐	☐
I am overlooked	☐	☐	☐
I don't feel I am appreciated	☐	☐	☐
I am poor	☐	☐	☐
I am lonely	☐	☐	☐
I fight with anger	☐	☐	☐
I am out of tune	☐	☐	☐
I don't feel good about my body	☐	☐	☐
I don't feel respected	☐	☐	☐
I don't see God at work	☐	☐	☐
I don't trust in Jesus Christ	☐	☐	☐
I don't pray	☐	☐	☐

A guide if the majority of your ticks fall into the categories above.

Sometimes	This is quite normal. Don't worry.
Often	You may well be anxious or potentially so. It would be a good idea to talk things through with someone you can trust.
Always	This is serious. Counselling or medical advice is essential.

Path out of Anxiety

	Sometimes	Often	Always
I accept myself	☐	☐	☐
I appreciate others	☐	☐	☐
I am blessed	☐	☐	☐
I love others	☐	☐	☐
I care	☐	☐	☐
I am at peace	☐	☐	☐
I am loved	☐	☐	☐
I enjoy life	☐	☐	☐
I am confident	☐	☐	☐
I am protected	☐	☐	☐
I am growing in faith	☐	☐	☐
I see God at work	☐	☐	☐
I have so much	☐	☐	☐
I am joyful	☐	☐	☐
I am positive	☐	☐	☐
I am expectant	☐	☐	☐
I like being helpful	☐	☐	☐
I love God	☐	☐	☐
I love my partner	☐	☐	☐
I like praying	☐	☐	☐
I am content	☐	☐	☐
I am not afraid of the future	☐	☐	☐

A guide if the majority of your ticks fall into the categories above.

Sometimes	You are quite normal. Don't worry. There is scope for development.
Often	You are very fortunate. Keep growing.
Always	You must be brilliant. Have you been totally truthful about yourself?

12 Tips For Overcoming Personal Anxiety

1. Take Regular Exercise.

The Apostle Paul's comment offered in a different context is still true: 'The spiritual did not come first, but the natural, and after that spiritual' (1 Corinthians 15:44). Feelings of anxiety may well have their roots in a low physical condition. Christians often treat their bodies like second class citizens. Eating healthily and taking regular exercise such as walking, cycling or swimming several times a week will quickly tone up your body and increase your alertness.

2. Worship Daily.

Look for passages of scriptures which describe God's marvellous acts, explore the names and character of God and turn these into song and prayers of thanksgiving. Thank him for what He has done for you; this is one sure way to see off anxiety. Don't worry if your singing isn't tuneful — only you and God are listening and He has wide musical tastes! There is great value in praying, praising and singing out loud, it can lift your soul to God and *in the process, you will feel good*.

3. Meditate on the Scriptures.

Worship isn't just about speaking to God but also listening to Him. One of the best ways in which you can do this is by meditating on the Bible. We have already dealt with this in some detail in the last chapter of this book, so go over that passage again and put it into practice.

4. Learn to Relax.

You can reduce stress by lying down on your back, on the floor, consciously wiggling your toes and telling your body to relax. Let this process go on as you mentally move up through your body (legs, torso, back, arms, neck and head). Listening to worship tapes or other soothing music can be a great help. It is also helpful to listen to tapes of Scripture being read.

5. Plan Ahead.

Avoid unnecessary stress by adjusting your schedule and avoiding the pile up of work or unforced deadlines. Plan break times and opportunities for relaxation into your programme — if work is allowed to pile up, healthy breaks will be the first priorities to bite the dust, whereas experience suggests there is all the more reason to maintain them.

6. Delegate.

As part of your planning ahead, determine to delegate non-essential tasks as far as possible. Even busy Mums can get the children to help them with household tasks. It may be more difficult to begin with but, once a pattern is established and they understand they are contributing to your well being, things become easier.

7. Avoid inter-personal conflicts.

Personal conflict adds to the anxiety burden; try agreeing with somebody, life should not be a constant battleground. Ask yourself whether there is any unresolved blame or unforgiveness. Bring those difficult relationships, both past and present, to the Lord and refuse to harbour grudges and grievances.

8. Keep clear of short term fixes.

Such as alcohol, tobacco and drugs, excessive credit and compulsive eating. Get enough sleep; sleeping pills may become unnecessary if you change your lifestyle.

9. Work within your capabilities.

Refuse responsibilities you cannot handle while being willing to stretch yourself a little. Ask yourself — in which areas are you not coping. Make a list and talk to somebody you trust.

10. Think of others.

Try to encourage or bless someone else every day. By removing the focus on yourself, the sense of anxiety is reduced.

11. Confess sin.

Deal with negative and enslaving habits through confession and prayer; be honest with and about yourself. Find a friend with whom you can discuss these needs and who can be a spiritual encourager in your life.

12. Accept yourself.

Make this well known prayer your own:

> *God grant me the serenity*
> *to accept the things*
> *I cannot change,*
> *Courage to change*
> *the things I can,*
> *And the wisdom to know*
> *the difference.*

Authors' Personal Profile

Dr Dick Whitehouse

Dick is the leader of Living Streams Ministries Trust whose motto is 'Equipping God's people for works of service'. Converted in the Methodist Church and brought up as a young Christian in the Christian Brethren, Dick enjoyed a crisis experience of the Holy Spirit whilst serving in the British Army. On leaving the army he worked as a youth evangelist in Wales before studying for one year at the Bible Training Institute in Glasgow. He then transferred to the London Bible College graduating with a Bachelor of Divinity degree.

Dick went into teaching to pay the bills while he pastored small churches. In the process he also studied part time to gain an M.Litt. in theology and an Advanced Certificate in Education. He later studied full time to obtain a doctorate in Sociology of Education.

After 16 years in Baptist pastorates, Dick pioneered a House Church in London and has since gone on to church pioneering work in Wales where he now lives with his wife, Margaret and their three children. During his time in Wales he has worked as publicity director for 'Tell Wales with Luis Palau'. The journalism skills which he acquired in the process have since been put to use as communications co-ordinator for Trans World Radio and as the Editor of the Evangelical Missionary Alliance's world missions digest called 'Facts Magazine'.

Dick has a monthly missions magazine programme on short-wave radio with TWR and edits 'Windows of Opportunity', an occasional newspaper published for AD 2000.

Rev L Gwynn Devey

Brought up in Pennsylvania, Gwynn served in the United States navy in the South Pacific towards the end of World War II when his commitment to Christ deepened. After the war he studied at Cincinnati Bible Seminary before going on to study medicine in San Jose where he received a bachelor's degree in Medical Science.

Following graduation, Gwynn served in a variety of pastorates firstly with the Church of Christ and then with the Baptists. During his pastorate in Healdsberg, northern California, he hosted a prime time television magazine style programme based on biblical exegesis and interviews with church leaders. His longest pastorate was with Sunset Baptist Church, San Francisco, where he also served as Chaplain to Teen Challenge. Whilst in San Francisco he broadcast regularly on the KEAR-FM radio station.

In the last years of his pastoral activity Gwynn served with the Florida Convention of the Southern Baptists and he was Regional Director of Family Life for the north of Florida. Gwynn has been a conference speaker in the USA and Britain particularly at the Southwold Convention and with the House Church movement.

Now retired from pastoral ministry, Gwynn lives with his wife Lorna, in Lake Wales, Florida. They have one son David who lives in California.

Bibliography and Selective Reading List

Anxiety in Christian Experience, Wayne E. Oates, Westminster Press, Philadelphia, 1955.

Constructive Aspects of Anxiety, Seward Hiltner & Karl Menninger, Abingdon Press, New York, 1963.

Designer Living: The Way to Beat Stress, Bill Munro, Monarch, Eastbourne, 1991.

Desiring God, John Piper, IVP, Leicester, 1989.

Disorders of the Emotional and Spiritual Life, W. L. Northridge, Channel Press, New York, 1961.

Emotional Maturity, Leon J. Saul, J. B. Lippincott & Co., Philadelphia, 1947.

Guilt and Grace, Paul Tournier, Harper & Row, New York, 1959.

Happiness is a Choice, Frank B. Minirth & Paul D. Meier, Baker Book House, Grand Rapids, 1978.

Inside Out, Lawrence J. Crabb, Navpress, Colorado Springs, 1988.

Living with Depression and Winning, Sarah Fraser, Tyndale House, Wheaton, 1975.

Overcoming Anxiety, Gary R. Collins, Vision House, Santa Ana, California, 1973.

The Practice of Godliness, Jerry Bridges, Navpress, New Malden, 1987.

Roots and Shoots, Roger Hurding, Hodder, London, 1986.

Spotlight on Stress, Gary R. Collins, Vision House, Ventura, California, 1983.

Stress: the Challenge of Christian Caring, Gaius Davies, Kingsway, Eastbourne, 1988.

The Transformation of the Inner Man, John & Paula Sandford, Victory House, Tulsa, 1982.

Telling Yourself the Truth, William Backus & Marie Chapian, Bethany House, 1980.

Whatever Became of Sin?, Karl Menninger, Bantam Books, New York, 1979.